The Art of Sensitive Parenting

Vedana

The Art of Sensitive Parenting

Samvedana

Amita Govinda

Publishers
Pustak Mahal®

J-3/16 , Daryaganj, New Delhi-110002
☎ 23276539, 23272783, 23272784 o *Fax:* 011-23260518
E-mail: info@pustakmahal.com o *Website:* www.pustakmahal.com

Sales Centre

- 10-B, Netaji Subhash Marg, Daryaganj, New Delhi-110002
  ☎ 23268292, 23268293, 23279900 o *Fax:* 011-23280567
  E-mail: rapidexdelhi@indiatimes.com
- 6686, Khari Baoli, Delhi-110006
  ☎ 23944314, 23911979

Branches

Bengaluru: ☎ 080-22234025 o *Telefax:* 080-22240209
E-mail: pustak@airtelmail.in o pustak@sancharnet.in
Mumbai: ☎ 022-22010941, 022-22053387
E-mail: rapidex@bom5.vsnl.net.in
Patna: ☎ 0612-3294193 o *Telefax:* 0612-2302719
E-mail: rapidexptn@rediffmail.com
Hyderabad: *Telefax:* 040-24737290
E-mail: pustakmahalhyd@yahoo.co.in

ISBN 978-81-223-1360-4

Edition: 2012

Printed at : Param Offsetters, Okhla, Delhi

Contents

Acknowledgements

It was in the year 1998 that the journey of Samvedana began. It emerged as a column addressed to parents in the newsletter, Dialogue, and focused on issues of child development and parenting with a view to developing common understanding between parents and teachers regarding children. I thank Gyan Bharti School which was instrumental in bringing out this newsletter. I take this opportunity to thank Mr. R.C. Shekhar who took keen interest not only in having it published regularly but also actively participating in critically reading it and giving suggestions. I wish to express my gratitude to the teachers and parents, whose regular interactions – formal and informal discussions about the problems that they faced in dealing with children – helped me in identifying the issues for Samvedana. Their constructive feedback and appreciation kept my enthusiasm for writing this column for almost a decade. I am grateful to Ms. Vatsala Zutsi who helped in editing Dialogue of which Samvedana was a part. I thank Bhawna Bhardwaj who readily agreed to do the illustrations, bringing to life the issues I have written about. I also thank all the children whose drawings and photographs have become a part of Samvedana.

I thank all my friends who not only inspired but also helped me in bringing out Samvedana in the form that it has taken now. In particular, I wish to thank Professor Namita Ranganathan, Central Institute of Education, University of Delhi, who meticulously went through the manuscript and helped me in editing it. She has been a dear friend and kept up my morale for publishing this work. I also express my deep gratitude to Dr. Anjana Mangalagiri for going through the manuscript and making very valuable suggestions. It is indeed her persuasive effort that helped me give final shape to the book. She injected life into this project at a time when it was beginning to languish.

I thank my family for always supporting me, and for finding meaning in what I write. My biggest debt of gratitude is to Govinda for being there always, for going through each issue of Samvedana, for giving his intellectual inputs, for the discussions and reflections that have finally taken the shape of this book. This book would not have been possible without him! I thank Radhika with whom I grew up and learnt the lessons of child rearing! Many of her anecdotes are even now etched in my mind and amuse me as I recall them. I thank her for assisting me in this endeavour. I thank Shishir for patiently helping me digitize the illustrations and photographs, and for eagerly listening to my ideas about this book. Thanks to Dilipbhai who showed a keen interest in the publication of this work. I thank Kumud Choksi who taught me to live life to its fullest by setting an example with her own. I express my heartfelt thanks to her for reading the manuscript, for her constant encouragement, and for having been a part of the journey that has culminated in this book.

About the Book

This book is about the Samvedana of parenting. Samvedana is the Hindi derivative of the Sanskrit root Sam-vedana, meaning feeling with deep sensitivity. This book uses the concept of Samvedana to underline the obligation of sensitive parenting and calls for creating an adult-child relationship of 'feeling together' in favour of the growing child. It is about exploring the physical and social/emotional world of the child with the child, in understanding the issues of child development. It opens up the child's world to the adult, both the parent and the teacher, a world that has been little understood and much misinterpreted. In doing so, it provides simple but valuable techniques to parents and teachers in handling children in early stages of schooling. The book is not only about the significance of sensitivity to children's growing needs but also about growing up with children. It is about understanding their conflicts and traumas at each phase of their development and facilitating them to resolve these. It invites parents to enjoy the fascinating journey of childhood and to relive it with the growing child. It thus evokes the samvedana of parenting – to understand children's perspectives in a sensitive manner, to listen to their side of the story, to be open to learn from them and to discover the profoundness of the inner child beyond what seems like flippant, external childishness.

The book is based on the work of the author with a number of schools and non-governmental organizations involved in implementing or promoting innovative preschool and primary education. Each issue dealt with in the book has been the subject of discussion with parents and teachers in a number of interactive sessions over the years. Many of the themes were revised based on the feedback from parents and teachers. All the ideas are based on real life experiences and personal narratives of cases from urban and rural schools with which the author has been associated over a span of more than two decades as a mentor and researcher. Advice that the book contains for teachers and parents is that which has been reported to have worked well for them.

Every parent would like to see her or his child grow into a balanced person realizing her/his full potential. Parents look for scientific but simple and easy to understand advice from real life. This is precisely what the book attempts to do – to reach out to the parents and teachers who are engaged in bringing up children. The most important characteristic of the book is its simple style and language. It avoids unnecessary theory and technical jargon and does not demand any specialized knowledge; yet, it is based on scientific evidences and has the potential to influence teachers and parents making them more sensitive to the growing child's cognitive, social and emotional needs. Built mainly on real life cases from their own surroundings, it has ready appeal to parents and teachers alike.

Finally, the book is unique in that it explicitly links home and school, work of parents and teachers, treating child's life space as one continuum between the home and the school. Thus, the proposed book traverses between home and school, addressing a critical group of modern parents whose children have just begun going to school. In this way, the book acts as a link between the parents and the teachers, contributing to development of a shared understanding of the challenges of dealing with the growing child. It attempts to bridge the traditional gaps in knowledge and expectations between the school and the home, which invariably affect the growth and development of the child. Yet, it is not unduly a problem-centered book; nor is it prescriptive, presenting to parents lists of dos and don'ts. It is crafted with a positive tone and language; it is more about helping teachers and parents alike to enjoy the playfulness, spontaneity and creativity of the growing child. Through this, the book tries to introduce to parents and teachers the principles and practices of 'sensitive parenting' or parenting with feeling.

To Teachers and Parents

Parents and teachers play an important role in the early stages of a child's life. The child is 'born' in the home with the school as an extension of the home. The kind of experiences, both pleasant and unpleasant, that the child has during the early stages set the tone and tenor for later development. A sense of security is a basic prerequisite for all aspects of development. Therefore, the social and emotional environment provided to the child becomes a critical factor influencing the child's course of learning and development.

There is a teacher in every parent and a parent in every teacher. Parents are the first teachers in a child's life. Before formal learning begins in school, children have already gone through an immense process of learning at home. They acquire behaviour patterns, habits and values demonstrated by their parents. Parents are their role models. A child's life is a continuum from home to school where teachers take on the role of substitute parents. Children expect the same nurturing and caring response from teachers. It is therefore important that parents and teachers complement each other's role to enable children to develop integrated personalities.

This book is for parents, teachers and people working with children to develop a common understanding about a growing child. It will help parents and teachers to understand the processes of child development, individual differences in developmental milestones and age appropriate tasks to infuse in children a sense of achievement rather than a fear of failure.

The feeling of success in children makes them confident individuals. In some of the chapters such as on 'Building Creative Spaces for Children', 'The Learning Child', 'The Child and the School,' age-appropriate activities are suggested to help parents and teachers design activities that can be carried out with children. Working together with children helps children grow healthy, both physically and emotionally. Adults' participation and involvement in children's activities help children to get the message that people around them are trustworthy. This makes them happy and secured.

I. The Growing Child

'The Growing Child' attempts to capture the different facets of the developmental journey that every child undergoes. In this journey, meeting the basic needs of the growing child occupies a central place. As the child grows, his or her world expands from family and home to school and the outside world. The focus is to clarify the various development stages and processes that form part of growing up for every child. The attempt is also to underscore the importance of the human context characterizing the growing child's life space – parents, grandparents and siblings and explore how these significant factors influence child's growth and development. The focus is also on suggesting ways of creating healthy relationships with mutual love and respect between the growing child and other members of the family which would have a lasting influence on the growth process.

I. The Needs of Young Children

II. Understanding the Social World of the Child

III. Let Us Make Eating Nutritious Food a Pleasant Experience for Our Children

IV. Developing Independence in Children

V. Growing Up with Siblings

VI. Grandparents – A Part of Child's Life Space

VII. Responding to Children's Questions

The Needs of Young Children

Why does my child cry? This is the agony of a perplexed mother on the first day of her child going to school. Some children take their own time to adjust to the new environment. And yet, you may find some children quite relaxed consoling others. What could be the reasons? The answers may not fully lie with the school. They are often linked to the child's experience of satisfaction or deprivation of his/her basic needs. What are the basic needs of a young child as a growing and developing person?

Physical wellbeing is important for all children. Children should receive proper physical care, an adequate and well balanced diet, suitable clothing, sufficient sleep, rest and exercise. It should be the concern of every parent and teacher to help children develop into healthy individuals. Physiological needs of children cannot be satisfied in isolation. For instance, you must have experienced your child demand that you carry him/her although he/she can walk independently. It is not that they are lazy but they look for attention, warmth and care of people around them. It is an attempt to satisfy their basic needs.

Security and acceptance are part of children's socio-emotional needs that provide the foundations for their future development. Children require continuous and consistent love from people around them. This love is best expressed in the early years by direct physical contact, by being responsive, and also by satisfying their need for food.

This helps them to become secure and confident individuals. Children need a nurturing environment where they are cared for, loved, accepted and encouraged. The satisfaction of socio-emotional needs helps them to develop a basic trust in people around them and experience a sense of belongingness. It is only when they are feeling secure within themselves that they begin to establish satisfactory relationships with people around them. Emotional stability is one of the greatest influences in a child's ability to learn. Children develop confidence in the world around them and in people, if their needs are met.

At this stage, the cognitive needs of young children are to explore and experiment with things in the environment and master basic skills. Exploration, which forms the basis of learning, is through the five senses. They need an environment which will arouse and satisfy their curiosity; they need problems to be solved. If these challenges are presented to them at the right time, in a way to ensure some measures of success, they become happy children.

How do we meet basic needs of children?

- The child is born into a family. It is the members of the family who provide satisfaction to the basic needs of children. For young children, school is an extension of their home, so the responsibility lies with the teachers at school as well.

- Parents at home and teachers at school need to provide a nurturing environment. Children need to get love, care and warmth. This will help in building up a sense of security and acceptance. Research on children has shown that a secure child tends to be happy, active and confident while an insecure child tends to be fearful, dependent and low in self-esteem.

- Taking care of physiological needs such as a balanced diet, proper rest, sleep and exercise help in the physical well-being of children. If these needs are satisfied, children develop into healthy, happy children.
- We need to provide a stimulating environment where children get the opportunity to express freely, explore the environment, and get appropriate material, attention and care.
- Parents and teachers should know about these basic needs of children so that they are able to respond appropriately.

Understanding the Social World of the Child

The urge to socialize, and to relate to others, is apparent from the earliest stage of a child's existence. The need to relate to other human beings is a basic need. Even the youngest infant demands not only to be dressed or fed, but also to be lifted, hugged, and fondled. In the beginning, it is the mother who is the key 'other person'. This world of the 'other' however expands as the child grows.

A child's social contact begins when she recognizes people who smile at her. But the interactive phase of her social world begins as she grows and starts playing with others. Two-year-old children may not really play together. Often you will see several children around a sand box, each one completely absorbed in what he or she is doing, and paying no attention to the others around. They accept the presence of others as long as there is no interference with what they are doing. The three year olds, in contrast, begin to enjoy being with other children of their age.

Although a child may forget the first playmates he/she had, they would have made an impact on his/her development. It is through them that the child learns to appreciate the rights and interests of others. These early experiences are likely to shape her social relationships as she grows. If the experiences are happy and joyful, she would not be fearful about meeting other friends. Also, it builds a foundation for emotional stability. She accepts differences between people and learns to accept defeat without flying into a rage.

Why does a child search for friends of her own age? Through friends of their own, children are more apt to learn to share. Having friends of the same age means more competition in games, and less domination or bossing by one person. Friends are the very breath of life for young children. They need other children to play with. They want to climb, run around, and to dress up together. No child is as happy as the one who has several friends of his/her own age.

There are some necessities in children's development that require interaction with co-equals, that is individuals who have the same kind of developmental status, and competencies in the cognitive and social areas, as they do. It is largely through the child's interaction with peers that many of his/her life's most important attitudes and behaviours are shaped. It is the peer experience that helps transform the egocentric child into a person with social consciousness and moral sensitivity.

Some of the social traits are gained by copying or modeling the behaviour of peers. Children often look for psychological support from close friends, particularly at critical times. This is because, it is in the peer group that they find others functioning at their own level of intellectual and emotional development, and come across human beings with whom they can interact as equals, comparing their perceptions of life and sharing their stresses and conflicts.

From their interactions with friends, children psychologically come to know that they are not alone, and that their occasional strange feelings of isolation, or fear, or aggression are shared by others.

What can we do as parents and teachers?

- We need to encourage them to choose their own peer group and interact with them. Some children prefer to play with older or younger playmates. This is quite natural. We may introduce new friends to them but should not impose friendships.

- For the child, his/her social world does not consist only of children but includes adults as well. Thus, we are part of their social world along with their peer group. For us, the adult world and child world may appear distinct, but for children it is seen as one world.
- Children do have their own stars and idols and their own cliques. This should not be viewed as a problem.
- As in other areas, children also acquire social behaviour by imitating adult behaviour within the family or by observing their peers whom they admire. It is this which places responsibility on parents and teachers to offer desirable behaviour patterns for them to emulate.

Let Us Make Nutritious Food a Pleasant Experience for Children

Lakshmi, the mother of five-year-old Balu, complains about her son fussing over food and not eating properly.

Vibha is upset about her daughter, who is six-year-old and throws up food whenever she drinks milk in the morning.

Montu's parents feel that their children eat potato chips and chocolates, instead of eating normal food.

This problem may not be of only these parents. You may also be facing similar kinds of problems with your children. Let us try to understand these problems and help our children to overcome them, and enjoy eating nutritious food.

Refusal to eat may often be an attention seeking behaviour. Some children take a lot of time to eat, fuss about food, demand for substitutes, or ask for less quantity of food. This is because these have proved to be helpful in keeping one, or both parents attending to them. The type of attention they attract may be pleasant or unpleasant but by doing this they ensure that they are not being ignored.

Forced feeding by anxious parents results in food being unpleasantly associated with anger, fear, unreasonable demands and tension. It is not surprising that many children throw up milk in the morning when it is given to them forcibly. You have to try out alternatives to match your child's taste. Insistence upon certain type and amount of food may create resistance to eating in general.

It is a common practice among many parents to use food as a reward or punishment for good or bad behaviour. Parents often reward children with chocolates, candies, and cookies when they behave as instructed, though these are not considered as nutritious food. Having nurtured such expectations and habits, parents should not be surprised if their children prefer sweets and chocolates to other food items. Similarly, depriving a child of food as a punishment can result in the child overvaluing food as a symbol of acceptance by the parents.

Some children have the tendency to overeat and some others have the problem of erratic eating. Overeating may lead to obesity in children. However, all obesity may not be linked to overeating. In many cases, it is genetic and related to endocrine imbalance. Wherever the problem of overeating and erratic eating is not linked to physiological disorders, parents have to carefully counsel the child. In most such cases, the problem disappears on its own with some help from the parents as the child grows up.

Some parents give a lot of importance to a child's table manners. Instead of allowing the child to enjoy his/her food, they nag all the time for being messy, slow, or clumsy in using a spoon and fork. Such an atmosphere is hardly conducive for enjoying food. The more pleasant and relaxed the eating experience is the faster will the child acquire socially acceptable habits in terms of what they eat and how he/she eats.

Children love to participate in the activities done by their parents at home. If we try to involve them in preparing food items, or any activity related to it, it can help to develop a sense of achievement and enthusiasm to eat those items. Also, most of these habits are acquired through observing others, including the eating habits and behaviour of adults at home. Merely exhorting that nutritious food is necessary for the growing child but not for grown up adults will not be convincing enough to children.

For children, it is a delightful experience to eat with their parents. This is the time when the parents can share their own experiences with their children, guide them in their behaviour and shape their food habits. How many of us make it a point to have at least one meal together with our children? Eating is not just to satisfy our physiological need, it also plays a very important role in establishing emotional bonds. It is this emotional relationship that can influence the children's eating behaviour, much more than mere rational advice on eating a balanced diet.

Developing Independence in Children

Every child has a strong desire to be independent. However, they look for a security cover from parents as they search for independence. Watch a small child run away from his parents. He runs a little way and then turns and looks back. He turns and looks back trying to spot his mother or father. If the parents smile reassuringly, the child runs away further and explores. He is learning that it is alright to go away on his own. He ensures that his parents approve of it. A wonderful bit of self-learning!

Very often, we hear children say, "I want to do it myself." It shows their urge to be independent. They want to show that they can do things for themselves. They can dress, eat independently and are able to manage their day-to-day chores. For them, there is always something new to discover and something new to try out. Sometimes, their desire to do things independently comes in conflict with what others want them to do. This is the stage where they experience conflict between dependency needs and the need for autonomy. In such situations, children typically try to avoid taking initiative in order to overcome the feeling of insecurity and guilt. When the child's desire to do things independently is supported by parents without creating a feeling of insecurity, he/she gets a sense of achievement and develops confidence in his/her abilities. Parents have to be sensitive and play a supportive role towards their child in facilitating this process of becoming independent.

In the process of growing up, everyone needs freedom to choose and act independently. Children too try to discover what it means to be independent and to be no longer entirely helpless and dependent on adults. They want to take decisions on their own but are often not sure of the consequences. They thus look for support from their parents. They try, at times, to follow their peer group. However, they may not like to move away from parents completely. Consequently, they experience conflict when their expectations and priorities do not match those of their parents. Achieving a favourable ratio of independence and dependence is the second basic task in healthy personality growth.

It is not easy to develop feelings of independence when one is compelled to be dependent on others. In such situations, some children develop a tendency to depend on others. They become afraid of becoming independent in their behaviour and thinking. In some special cases, such continued dependence may arise out of unfavourable physical conditions and illnesses like asthma, diabetes, or disability from an accident. However, in most cases, it significantly depends on their home environment where perhaps independent behaviour is consistently discouraged. How well one succeeds in achieving this balance in early life will, in a large measure, determine the kind of adult a child will become.

How do we help them become independent?

We have to realize that we are dealing with children who are growing physically, socially, emotionally and intellectually. Children gradually acquire the ability to use their bodies in ways which make it easier for them to be independent in walking, reaching out, climbing, dressing up and performing other daily chores.

We could help them by getting them clothes that they can manage themselves so that they begin to dress and undress without help. We could get them play material that they can manipulate without having to ask for help. We could keep their things at places within their reach so that they do not have to ask for help.

Watch for signs that indicate the urge to be independent. Listen for words like 'let me do it' and 'I can do it for myself.' Convey the message that they can do things for and by themselves and that you value their being independent. Developing a sense of autonomy gives them the confidence that they would be able to eventually handle situations and events that are likely to happen later in their lives.

We have to give them opportunities to do their daily chores independently. This builds confidence in their abilities to look after themselves and also gives them a sense of achievement.

There are individual differences between children. Some become independent at an early age. They do their tasks with minimal help while others may need more help. Of course, every child would like to be in the lap of his/her mother. This gives them a sense of security. They do need periodical reassurance of feeling safe and being loved. If children seek such reassurance, do not interpret it as their being over-dependent.

In order to develop independence, we have to respect the individuality of children. They should not be treated either as babies, or as mature adults. One should not expect them to be dependent at all times nor expect adult standards of behaviour from them. It is essential for adults to have trust and confidence in children's growing independence. Give them reassurance about their ability to carry out tasks independently and take their own decisions. As they grow older, this can be done by involving them and considering their opinions in taking decisions about affairs which concern them.

Growing up with Siblings

"Mama, he is pulling my hair. I will beat him," cries the daughter. "But he is small. You cannot hurt him," responds the mother. This is a common feature in many households. How should the mother respond to such situations? This is not sibling rivalry but a passing phase. However, parents need to handle such situations with care and understanding.

Siblings spend most of their time together and share a wide range of activities. The kind of relationship that siblings share among themselves has an everlasting influence on their personality. The relationship is complex. They can be playmates and companions. There is solidarity and security. At the same time, one may find them fighting, being jealous of one another, and developing feelings of insecurity. They often love, hate, cooperate, try to control or resist each other. It is a part of the growing up process.

Lalita is worried about her five-year-old daughter Nilu who is very possessive of her little sister. She does not allow anyone else to play with her. Most of the time she expresses fear that something may happen to her sister and that she has to protect her sister.

Seven-year-old Jay is a very quiet child. Parents often talk about his elder sister who is outgoing and does well in studies. Although there is a large gap between the two siblings, they do not seem to get along well.

Fourteen-year-old Rima often feels that her brother who is much younger to her is given more freedom than her.

She argues with her parents that they are biased and do not treat her as a grown up girl.

Sibling relationships are influenced by many aspects – birth order, age, sex, spacing of children, and family size. They are all interrelated. Parental attitudes and behaviour towards their children are crucial in developing a healthy relationship. No parent would want to encourage jealousy among siblings but they may unconsciously contribute to it by comparing them or treating them differently because of their gender.

Sometimes, through comparison, they communicate to the younger one that he has to live up to the standards set by the older sibling in scholastic achievement and other aspects of behaviour.

In the case of Jay, he is always compared with his older sibling. Consequently he seems to become withdrawn. The relationship with the older sibling alternate between companionship and rivalry. Younger children enjoy being with their older siblings and turn to them for protection and help but they also resent the privileges that the older siblings enjoy and compete with them for attention and approval.

In Nilu's case, though outwardly she is possessive of her sister, she may essentially be conveying her own feelings of insecurity. Probably by obstructing others, she tries to get all the attention instead of her sister. Parental expectations and demands toward the first-born child are raised and increased by the arrival of the second child. Parents generally demand more independent behaviour from the first born. Jealousy arises out of this expectation and the feeling of being deprived. Younger children always enjoy what older children have had to relinquish, particularly, attention from adults.

While they may recognize the advantages and privileges of being older, they also want the advantages and privileges of being the 'baby'. First born children resent the loss of whatever helpless, baby behaviour they enjoyed and may attempt to hold on to those previous behaviour patterns that they associate pleasantly with dependency.

Rima's case seems to be more complex. It is not uncommon that parents treat girls and boys differently. This may seem 'natural' for the parents but not necessarily for the children. With no clarification coming from the parents except the standard statement, 'he is a boy and you are a girl', it is natural for Rima to think that her parents have a special love for her brother, which she does not enjoy.

Every child wants a good share of parental love, attention and affection. It is not an unnatural reaction for him/her to want to be the most important and to be the best. Every action of the parents is seen from such an angle. When children feel that they are not getting their share of parental love and understanding, their disadvantaged feeling causes them to become jealous.

To most children, sharing anything simply means getting less of it and may be charged with feelings of resentment and jealousy. When it is seen as losing parental attention, it complicates their feelings. In some cases, sharing leads to the development of love.

Rivalry among siblings is usual in any culture. Conflicts and fights occur but they tend to be short lived. Siblings serve as mirrors, sounding boards and testing grounds for each other. They can make life difficult or easy for each other. They can be supportive and provide a sense of security, or be obstructive and create a feeling of threat.

We all harbor some jealous feelings. A certain amount of jealousy is normal, but not in its extreme forms. It may become a hindrance for the growth and development of children, if they are constantly preoccupied with jealous feelings. As a result, they may suffer from poor self-image, and fail to form and sustain good peer relationships.

Promoting healthy sibling relationships

- Parents and children spending time together as a family is a basic requirement for developing healthy sibling relationships.

- Preparing the older child mentally for the birth of the second child will help. But remember that the first born still needs the attention and love of parents.
- Treat each child as a special individual so that the older sibling does not take the burden of being the 'responsible person' all the time.
- Assign age appropriate responsibilities and privileges to each sibling so that each knows what is expected and there is no room for competition.
- If parents have reasons to treat children differently, due to their age or gender or capability, it is essential that these reasons are discussed openly with children when they are together.
- Try to understand and accept the child's feelings of jealousy and rivalry while firmly limiting their violent expressions.

Grandparents – A Part of a Child's Life Space

Grandparents are an important part of children's lives with a huge potential to influence their growth and development. Grandparent-grandchild togetherness is not just another relationship in the family. Rather, it spans the generation cycle, giving to the child an opportunity to understand another view of life and bridging what is commonly referred to as the 'generation gap'. One would find reference to the grandparents in almost everything that the children do. You find them shown in the drawings of children and in the stories that they narrate. Quite often, when asked to draw their family, grandparents figure prominently in the drawings of many children. Of course, the people in the personal space of children keep changing and expanding as they grow, which gets reflected in the nature of their relationship with others around them, including their grandparents.

The kind of relationship that children develop with their grandparents is influenced by the pattern of family life, as well as by the attitudes and behaviour of different family members. These social relationship patterns within the family, in turn, influence the child's development. The relationship with grandparents depends on the closeness of emotional tie between them and their own parents. Studies show that children's relationship with grandparents keep changing as they grow older. Young children like indulgent grandparents.

Generally, one finds that children resent the presence of their grandparents if they show authority over them and become stricter than their own parents. On the other hand, if grandparents are mainly interested in fun sharing activities, they will be welcome members of the intimate circle of the child.

Many children are attached to their grandparents for a variety of reasons. In some homes, grandparents take responsibility for looking after them and thus develop a close relationship. Grandparents, who have ample time to pamper their grandchildren, may at times create discomfort at home. It is not unusual to find parents complaining of the difficulty they face when child rearing practices adopted by grandparents which do not match with the way they want to bring up their children. Yet, no one can deny the warmth added by grandparents to the life of a child in the early years.

How do we build grandparent – grandchild togetherness?

- Children are capable of building their emotional bond and relationship with their grandparents. Allow the relationship to evolve. Do not colour the child's views based on your relationship with their grandparents. Children are also capable of dealing with the rules of different homes. The child knows that in grandma's house, for instance, you cannot wear shoes inside the house and cannot watch television after dinner.

- It is normal for parents and grandparents to disagree on certain child care issues. After all, they grew up in different conditions and carry different memories of their own childhood.

- To avoid frictions, be clear and firm about your choices. Explain to your parents that they should have confidence in you for raising your child. Tell them that you are always open to their suggestions but that you will take advice from other sources also like doctors, experts, or from books.

- It is not easy to listen to constant directions or advice from others. Accept it as a well-meaning advice from somebody who cares for you. Be open and use whatever you think is right. At the same time, tell them about your views on contemporary parenting by engaging in dialogue and reading out articles and books together which concern children and their development.

- Very often, grandparents feel neglected in their own home and feel useless and worthless. This may get reflected in their general behaviour with others, including the grandchildren. Encourage and create opportunities for grandparent-grandchild bonding. Let them play, go out for a walk, read story books, and help each other in their daily chores. By doing this, grandparents get a sense of self-worth and a feeling of being a valued member of the family. The child, in turn, gets a feeling of security through the love and attention.

- If grandparents are not living together with you, make sure that your children get an opportunity to be with them during vacations, or other occasions.
- Your treatment of and behaviour with your parents demonstrates the pattern of behaviour to your child. If you do not treat your own parents with respect, children learn the same. Remember that imitation is a major mode of learning for the young child. Just by preaching to respect elders at home, children do not learn. It is very important that as adults we respect others, so that children imbibe the right value system.

Grandparent-grandchild relationship, indeed, gives to the child an intuitive understanding of history – not as the dead past but as a living phenomenon. If nurtured with mutual respect and love for each other, it can create a wonderful world of inter-generational space – grandparents, parents and children!

7

Responding to Children's Questions

Very often, parents are puzzled by the unending series of questions that children ask. It is not always easy to find the right answers. We all experience similar situations when we do not know what to answer and decide in how much detail we need to respond to our children. Let us read the following incidents.

The whole family was watching television. There was an advertisement of a new brand of a car moving very fast. The little boy was fascinated by this and asked what it was? The father gave a detailed account of different parts of the car and how it works. In no time, the boy got thoroughly bored and started yelling.

"Mama, tell me, where have I come from?" The mother was embarrassed but still replied to her daughter that she came from her tummy. The girl was not satisfied with her answer. The mother got irritated and told her to shut up. Further, she told her that she should not ask such silly questions.

Responding to children's questions may prove extremely difficult, causing irritation, embarrassment and frustration. The difficulty may be that the answer is beyond the comprehension of the child. The reaction also depends partly on the circumstances and the kind of questions asked. Some questions asked by children are easy to reply to. Probably most questions fall in this category. Generally they are 'What is that?' kind of questions. This helps children to build their vocabulary and expand their understanding of the things around them. For such questions, most parents are too happy to respond to their children's probing minds. But sometimes even very considerate parents may lose their patience when their children keep pestering them. It is hard to know how much, or what information to give children at different stages of their development. Too much information given to the child, invariably leads to boredom.

However, it is important that children get satisfactory answers to their questions. If children are constantly rebuked or stopped from asking questions, they may avoid interacting with adults and may even lose their self-confidence. Further, it kills their natural curiosity and enthusiasm. You may have observed that when little ones enter the kindergarten, they have a number of questions to ask. Normally, questions are indications of interest and enthusiasm. Children ask questions when they are interested in something. It is the expression of hunger for knowing, and this hunger has to be satisfied, if they have to grow intellectually. We should encourage them by our positive attitude and responses. Most thinking and learning in us grow out of such explorations. As children seek information, their questions reveal their ways of thinking.

In answering their questions, it is important to tell them the truth. In telling them the truth, even about unpleasant realities, we are not harming them but actually preparing them to adjust to the realities of life. Therefore, do not try to hide facts thinking that they are too young and that the truth may hurt them. It is often not the truth that hurts but the way it is presented.

Sometimes you may face situation involving controversies on the correctness of an answer. You as a parent may not be convincing enough in your answer, or may not be sure of the answer. In such cases it is best if parents and children search together in an encyclopedia, or any other appropriate reference book. With this, children learn to respect the authority based on knowledge, rather than opinions.

The age level of the child asking a question is an important guide to the type of response. What is natural curiosity to the child may be embarrassing for you. That does not, however, call for refusal to answer the question. For instance, children seeking information about their own body parts, or the behaviour of people around them should be answered truthfully, keeping in view the age of the child and their capacity to comprehend the information being given. Your refusal or avoidance will not stop them from seeking answers from unreliable sources, or even imagining wrong answers. A feeling of mutual confidence is very important, even in ordinary conversational relationships.

In young children, one finds very little difference between reality and their make believe world. Some children do believe, for instance, in Santa bringing gifts.

It is important that they develop early in life, a clear realization of the difference between what is real and what is imaginary. Your responses have to gradually lead them to develop this capacity to differentiate.

You must have experienced the eternal, 'Why is it so?' question of a four-yeal-old. Why is the sky blue? Why is that old man's face like that? Why does that bird have red dots? Often children do not wish to know 'why' in these situations. They are just trying to seek reassurance about whatever they have noticed is right or not. They are reporting their observations and want to find out whether you have noticed the same. In these cases they are generally satisfied by your recognition and approval.

Through questions children acquire different concepts. The process continues throughout life. They discover that questions are helpful not only to get information but also to find out causes and relationships. Teachers as well as parents should therefore build the habit of critical thinking.

Finally, treat all questions of your child with respect and seriousness even if they appear trivial. Never laugh at these queries. For the child every question is a very significant piece of knowledge that she is trying to discover or the assurance she is seeking.

2. Nurturing the Emotional Life of Children

The critical role of parents in the child's emotional life is the focus of this Chapter. It is well-known that the kind of environment provided to the child in the early stages of growth and development leaves a lasting impact on the child's personality. Warm and nurturing environment at home helps the child to grow to be an emotionally secure and confident individual. Children imbibe consciously or unconsciously a variety of inputs from the home environment that shapes their sense of right and wrong and an understanding of discipline. Positive language and an ambience of harmony are crucial for the child's development not only in their social and emotional aspects but also for their cognitive development. It is important that parents consistently give the message of unconditional love and a feeling of total security that they are there to support the child in any situation.

I. Parents in the Emotional Life of Children

II. Positive Language in A Child's Life

III. How Do Our Children Learn Right from Wrong?

IV. How Do We Instill Discipline in Children?

V. Let Us Make the Child's Life Simple and Straight

VI. Harmony at Home

VII. Mama, Do You Still Love Me?

Parents in the Emotional Life of Children

Children are expected to behave according to socially desirable patterns. But this does not always happen. Sometimes, we find our children behaving in peculiar ways. They may hit or bully others, or lie down flat on the floor and scream. We may also find that some children just sit alone and do not mix with others. Of course, in most cases, the set of undesirable behaviour wear off as the children grow older. Like many other emotional problems this may also be a passing phase of development, to be ignored. It is only if such behaviour persists and threatens to have harmful consequences on the growth and development of the child that one needs to feel concerned. Why does that happen at all? Can we help such children to channelize their behaviour in a more constructive way? Can we help to prevent it? What would that mean to parents?

Creating an atmosphere of trust and belongingness

As we all know, in the early stages of development, children's worlds are limited to their homes. It is there that they develop a sense of basic trust, provided they are accepted in the family. This, to a great extent, depends on how parents gratify their need for food, attention and love.

Many a times we hear parents reacting to their children's behaviour: ***'oh, mine is a cranky one; he is a real bully'***; or ***'she is a loner, she does not mix with anyone'***. But why is this so? The answer could possibly be in the behaviour of the adults at home!! Children become cranky perhaps because in their early childhood, they were not attended to properly. For instance, if the child had to cry every time to get food, he may, in course of time, develop it into a habit. Or, in other cases, continuous nagging and comparison to other children could have prompted the child to adopt withdrawn behaviour. *In yet another case, the child bullies others and hits them probably because he has always seen his parents fighting. The child invariably accepts the behaviour of parents as the model and tends to acquire similar attitudes and values.* Parents who use physical punishment to curb a child's aggression are actually encouraging it, providing a model of aggressive, destructive behaviour to be imitated. Of course, parents are not the only models for children. They learn certain behaviour from their siblings and peers as well. Mass media also provides children with models for acquiring such forms of undesirable behaviour.

An important aspect of parents' interaction with their children centers on their disciplinary style. The way in which parents use reward and punishment differs greatly. Controlling children through external force in the form of punishment symbolizes authoritarian behaviour. Many a times, due to strict rules and regulations at home, children develop fear of parents and develop a feeling of insecurity. This can lead to problems like becoming withdrawn or aggressive, and other disorders like thumb-sucking and bed wetting. The authoritarian/disciplinary style prevents children from recognizing their own potential and interferes with the development of their self-identity. Parents who provide a warm and nurturing environment to their children help them develop a positive self image and self-esteem. Such children are confident about their actions, feel emotionally secure, and develop a sense of belongingness which also helps them to develop a positive relationship with others.

Providing a positively stimulating environment

Parents can provide a stimulating environment at home to their children through different play situations such as painting, creative writing, music, and dramatization or through simple interaction with them. These activities

should be part of their daily life so that children get a natural outlet for externalizing their internal conflicts and confusions that may be bothering them.

This will also help prevent the emergence of emotional and behavioral disorders and help in the development of the total child, who is emotionally mature and balanced. It is not enough if parents provide their children with a variety of play materials like toys, blocks and puzzles. It is more important that they spend time with them and actively participate in the whole process of play, making it a joyful experience.

This will help in the development of imagination, creativity, problem solving, reasoning and so on. In play situations, children learn many lessons of life and prepare themselves for future roles. While playing, children not only learn the rules of the game but also learn such socially desirable behaviour as waiting for their turn, sharing, helping, cooperating, and making adjustments with others.

All children have some or the other potential in them. Parents have to tap their potential and encourage them, by providing guidance and opportunities.

Activities like painting and creative writing help them to take out their inner feelings and emotions and to come to terms with reality. Activities like sports and dancing help them to channelize their energy in a more constructive way.

Reading is another activity which can be introduced at an early age. Young children enjoy picture books of animals, birds and objects around them. Once they learn to read, they enjoy reading about them. Although their selection of reading material changes as they grow older, the interest developed in reading remains intact. Reading together with children helps in sharing ideas and appreciating the writings of others. It also helps in increasing their information and knowledge base and broadens their perspective.

What do young children expect from their parents and teachers? If they could really articulate, they would perhaps say the following:

We want our parents and teachers

- to provide warm and nurturing environment at home and school
- to listen to us and have a dialogue instead of instructing us on dos and don'ts
- to be sensitive to our feelings
- to help us in attaining social and emotional maturity
- to be firm and consistent in their behaviour towards us
- to avoid comparisons with other children
- to avoid showing favouritism amongst us to set expectations according to our age and individual capacity.

2

Positive Language in A Child's Life

Let me start with a story, which depicts the influence of positive language on the emerging self-concept of children:

Once a teacher asked all her students to talk about the qualities of their classmates that impressed them the most... All of them talked about qualities they liked most in one another and how inspired they felt! The teacher compiled the list of qualities and gave each student a piece of paper wherein his or her qualities were written. They grew up and settled in different professions. One of those students had joined the army and had died in the war. A piece of paper, which he had treasured throughout his life, was found from his pocket. On the piece of paper was written, 'This was my inspiration'. Below were a few words in a different handwriting. Another student from the group, who met the teacher after several years, showed her the piece of paper and asked, 'Do you recognize the handwriting?'

In fact, most of her students had treasured that piece of paper as a pleasant memory – a gift of positive thinking. The qualities written on the piece of paper by the teacher had become a reference point for what each student believed about him/herself.

What does the story convey to us? Language has a powerful effect on a child's emotional life. Positive or negative messages transmitted during their childhood have long term implications. Many children carry pleasant memories of their childhood, while many others carry the scar of hurtful words from their childhood and live with a feeling of inadequacy. Very often, we hear negative statements from children describing themselves as: 'I am stupid, I cannot do it.' 'I am not cut out for that.' 'I am an ugly looking creature.'

The question is what made them think like this? Do we provide them positive and constructive feedback? What kind of language do we use? Let us reflect on these questions.

Use positive language whenever you can

In our daily lives, there are several occasions when we communicate in negative tones more easily when correcting children's behaviour. Using positive language instead and constructive feedback meets the same objective. At the same time, this helps children develop self-confidence and think positively about themselves. Try out for yourself the effect of each of these statements.

- You always leave behind a mess after playing OR I feel happy and proud when you put your toys away after playing.
- You never listen to me when I speak to you OR I would appreciate if you listened to me when I speak.
- You have nothing to do except watching TV OR Let us decide on what programme you will watch on TV.
- Do not disturb me. Don't you see that I am working? OR Will you give me some time? Let me finish this, and then I will attend to you.

Show children how to use positive language

Children learn the usage of language from adults – particularly parents, teachers and older siblings, imbibing their expressions, choice of words, the tone in which they speak from people around them. It is, therefore, important that we insist on positive language from everyone at home. If you think that your child is developing negative self-talk, do not reinforce it. Focus on your child's positive statements and ignore the negative ones for a while. It is easier to change behaviour by focusing on the positive aspects instead of the negative ones.

- o Help them learn to receive and give compliments.
- o Teach them how and when to say 'I appreciate ...' 'Thanks for your kind gesture.' 'I was touched by your...' 'I feel proud of ...' 'It was nice of you to think...' and so on.

Often children are not aware when they make negative statements about others. When your child says that her teacher is stupid, remind her that such remarks are not needed. It is alright if she does not like something in the teacher but that does not require her to make negative statements about her. The same could be expressed in a different manner.

We should help replace negative statements with positive ones. We have to make them realize that their words can hurt others. Help them appreciate that they can build mutual confidence and influence their own views and of others around them for the rest of their lives by using positive language.

It makes a meaningful difference when adults take the trouble to talk with children rather than at them. Adults' talk with children, whether a brief or a long exchange, is most useful when it takes account of the child's language ability. Spoken words as well as nonverbal messages can be used to communicate in a positive or negative manner depending on the age and stage of development of the child.

It is not that criticisms should never be made. But, remarks such as 'you are stupid' 'you are useless' or 'you are never going to learn' are not helpful to the child. They give no information to the child on how he/she could do better next time. Unless we provide reasons for the criticism or suggest how the child could manage what she is doing, such remarks only discourage the child and leave a sense of hurt in her. A good rule of thumb is to imagine how you, as an adult, would feel if someone dismissed your efforts with a derogatory remark. Children are not very different in their emotional reactions. They feel the same way as you do.

How Do Our Children Learn Right from Wrong?

Statements told to children such as 'good children listen to elders and do not argue...' marks the beginning of a long and gradual process of learning to behave in a socially approved manner. Just as physical, socio-emotional and intellectual development takes place in children over a period of time, moral development similarly has its own stages. Very young children do not have the concept of right or wrong. They simply obey rules laid down by adults. They judge their acts as right or wrong in terms of their consequences. They learn that they are expected to follow the rules, failing which, they will be punished, or will not get social approval.

Children begin conforming to the social expectations in order to gain rewards. They adopt good behaviour which may be seen by the adults as morally right. However, this does not help them differentiate clearly the 'right' and the 'wrong' behaviour. From ages five to eight, the rigid notions of right and wrong learnt from parents and other adults are gradually modified. Children begin to take into consideration the specific circumstances related to moral violations. For a five-year-old, lying is always bad but a slightly older child recognizes that lying is justified in some situations and is, therefore, not always bad. Later, children develop a conscience of their own. An action becomes right not because the society says it is right but because their conscience says so.

Children's growing sense of right and wrong behaviour is formed at home. It is from their family that children form their sense of values and learn the behaviour patterns that will guide them throughout their life. Within the family system, they discover what is expected of every individual, each of whom has a unique role. They learn those behaviours that are acceptable, and those that are not, those that are kept private and those that can be discussed openly. Day after day, they absorb and learn the pattern of behaviour shown to them.

What kind of an environment would help children make the right kind of moral choices?

- The most effective way of passing these ethical standards is simply living them. Children learn lessons in values by watching how adults live and interact with others. Everything we do becomes an example to follow. We are constantly demonstrating to them ethical standards by our daily behaviour, consciously or unconsciously. Being a role model for our children is not an option but a fact of life. We, therefore, need to be careful about what and how we model.

- As we are continuously confronted by the need to make moral choices in our daily lives, allow children to make choices as it is a crucial component of ethical behaviour. For example, a neighbour's child comes to borrow colour pencils and you tell your child to tell him that he does not have them although your child does. What happens to your child? The child is not only confused but also feels guilty about it.

Some children grow up to understand this as they develop reasoning ability and are able to handle the confusion. But some live with a perpetual sense of guilt affecting their mental health. The message is simple – there needs to be synchronization between what we preach and what we do.

- o Most children behave in appropriate ethical ways. We need to recognize and acknowledge this. By doing this, we are reinforcing their behaviour in a positive way. All children seek recognition which is a basic human need. If they cannot get it in a positive way, they are sure to get it by acting out negatively. We need to direct their behaviour towards the positive so that their behaviour and actions reinforce internal belief that their essential nature is one of goodness and value. It is, therefore, necessary to be aware of what behaviour we must praise. These could be simple events such as returning a toy that another child left accidently in your house, helping an old person cross the road, or showing kindness to a child in the class who is not keeping well.

- o Help children to have a positive self image so that their internal vision represents the picture of an ethical self that they can create. Tell them a story or read out the biographies of people whom you would like them to emulate. It helps them to form a picture of what an ethical person looks like, talks and acts. Children personalize that vision as a positive role model that they want to grow up into. In every era and in every culture, thinkers and spiritual people have recognized the basic truth that we become what we think about.

- o Create an open and non-judgmental environment at home. Children must know that any opinion they express will be listened to with respect and regarded as serious and thoughtful. Even when they are very young, we need to show respect for their own worth and value.

This is a healthy approach through which children can reach a clear position on moral questions. If they do not feel safe discussing with parents, they turn to their peer groups for resolving tough ethical choices which may not be desirable. Many families use the dinner table conversation as a forum for bringing up the ethical issues that affect our lives. By this, children and adults learn together the lessons of conflict resolution, negotiation and compromise.

- Rules must be the same for all family members. When rules are set up for the whole family, children imbibe appropriate behaviour in a natural manner. When adults do not abide by the same rules, it leaves children confused. The rules may be about the division of work at home or how many hours of watching T.V. are permissible. When all family members honour the joint decisions then there is integrity and respect for each other.

How Do We Instil Discipline in Children?

Ganesh is a four and a half year old happy child. Generally, he is engaged in play or some other activity of his own without disturbing others at home. But his mother is puzzled that whenever she has visitors he starts behaving in an awkward manner. He does not allow his mother to talk and at times, he even tends to be destructive.

Anmol, a nine-year-old, very often shouts and screams in the class. He constantly disturbs other children in the classroom. He does not allow others to work. At the playground, he hits others and bullies other children.

Rashu invariably comes back home late in the evening after play. This has become a constant point of tension at home in the evenings.

These are not stories from unusual homes but common occurrences in every home. All of us face situations when our children disobey us, behave in an unruly manner, throw tantrums and make us feel desperate and embarrassed. But in the normal course, most children outgrow such behaviour patterns. It should be a matter of concern if children continue to be indisciplined and destructive. How should we handle such situations?

How should we discipline?

All children need discipline. By discipline we mean direction and control of impulses. To be disciplined is to follow accepted norms of social behaviour. Children acquire such behaviour through a process of positive and negative feedback from adults. They begin recognizing what is socially acceptable and what is to be avoided. Parental acceptance and appreciation acts as the main tool of building discipline in children.

Good discipline is based on mutual respect and confidence. In many homes, in their anxiety to bring in disciplined behaviour, children are spanked and shamed when they misbehave or disobey. In the short term, we know that punishment of this kind may change the child's behaviour. However, it is likely to provoke impulses in the child which are difficult to manage in the longer term, particularly if it becomes a repeated phenomenon, setting in fear, resentment and the feeling of withdrawal in many children. The goal of good discipline has to be self-control, not external control.

Dealing with common problems of discipline

Exploring the reasons for particular events of indiscipline is very important. Often we jump to conclusions and generalize too quickly with phrases like: 'you have become a bully' or 'you want to deliberately hurt me'. Such outbursts can provoke children to also generalize: 'my parents do not love me anymore' and thereby set in motion a cycle of actions and reactions. We have to try and get out of such traps. For instance, Ganesh in the above case was trying to seek your attention without any intention to hurt your or the visitor's feelings. Unable to join in adult activity, children employ unusual ways of seeking attention and love.

Sometimes children may know what is expected of them but because they are busy or confronted with temptations, they forget to follow our expectations. This is what possibly happened in the case of Rashu. She would get engrossed in play and fail to return home in time. Gentle reminders can be given in several ways. Sometimes a mild warning can be sounded in advance. If such incidents persist, we must show our disapproval in a form that is clear to the children.

This usually means – a scolding, a stern 'no', or a withdrawal of privileges. It is important that they learn that their violation of rules is followed by unpleasant experiences. After such incidents, it is very important to take the first opportunity to let children know that you still love them and have confidence in them. It is a good practice to make sure that they are shown explicit affection before they go to bed.

Often the experience of lack of affection and love in the home environment could push a child to adopt unacceptable behaviour patterns, leading to being branded as a bully, an aggressive or maladjusted child and so on. Could this be the reason for Anmol's unacceptable behaviour in the classroom and on the playground? As parents, we sometimes presume that we are meeting the expectations of our children and wonder why they are not reciprocating our affection and love. We could, however, be wrong in our assumption. Just as we expect the child to listen to us, we too should have the time and patience to listen to what our children expects from us. They are generally not unreasonable. They may just want that we spend more time with them. The child may just want to tell us that he feels neglected or discriminated in comparison to his sibling.

When we are inconsistent, children are tempted to test our limits. They try to find out how far they can go. But when they know what is expected, they are likely to accept the limits as a dependable guide to action. Discipline is not a one way process that gives parents the right to dictate how children should behave. It has to be truly social and mutual. We have to understand and accommodate children's expectations in our behaviour too.

Disciplining involves both showing of love and displeasure. In many homes, however, parents drift into a damaging division of labour. The mother is indulgent, affectionate and permissive. The father is stern, unbending and demanding. This does not help. We have to recognize that there is no actual conflict between love and discipline. In fact, the best way to show our love to children is to help them gain self-control, to help them to live up to standards of conduct, appropriate to their age and social context. We can do this effectively and without hurting their self-esteem, if we build in them the feeling that we are also dependable sources of love and care.

When children misbehave in unacceptable ways, they need to learn how other people and we, as parents, feel about such behaviour. Mere punishment will not do. There are children who receive a great deal of punishment but very little discipline. It requires us to spend adequate time with our children and explain in simple ways how their behaviour could hurt others.

It is not just children who make mistakes. We get angry too and in the heat of the moment do things which later in moments of calm, we wish we had not done. Our children do recognize this human nature. If a child consistently receives consideration and love, such events are taken in his/her stride. In fact, we should ensure that our guilt and uncertainty will not make us so unsure of ourselves that we are unable to act naturally.

In good discipline, we let the child learn from experience and face consequences without any real harm. We need to help them get this sense of inner direction. The goal is to get children to take care of themselves and to develop a conscience that guides them when we are not around.

Let Us Make the Child's Life Simple and Straight

Mrs. S: The School does not teach. But I have taught my child who is in Nursery to write the alphabets and numbers.

Mrs. G: I do not think that is right. I just allow my son to do whatever he wants to do. He likes to colour and draw. Perhaps, it is better to follow what the teachers in the school tell us. We should not create contradictions in the child's mind.

Mrs. N: Perhaps, you are right. I spent a day in the school observing the children. That helped me understand the approach better. But when will my daughter learn alphabets and numbers?

Conversations like these amongst mothers of young children are not unusual. It reflects their concern and anxiety about their sons and daughters. This is natural. But it also tells us about the understanding that is gradually emerging among parents. Let us try to reflect a little more on the underlying substance of such conversations.

Home and school share a common responsibility to provide pleasant experiences to our children. We work towards the common goal of helping children in their total growth and development. The question is how should this goal be achieved in a pleasant and enjoyable manner? The child's happiness is the prime concern.

For us adults, school and home are two separate entities. But for the child, life at home and at school is one continuum, each day. Home to school is only an expansion of the social world, with more people around. Should we not build on this simple perception of the child, instead of imposing our adult understanding? The more we bridge the home-school distance in our mind and actions, the better it is for our children.

A child is born to the home but the process of growing up continues outside the home as well. For every child, the school is one such natural extension of home into the larger world. The child's learning and development process should be presented as a unified whole in line with the child's perception of the home-school continuum. In fact, the child finds in the teacher a parent-substitute and expects parental love, attention and feelings of security. It is only much later that the child differentiates the roles of parent and teacher. Yet the two remain an integral part of the environment, without any dichotomy. It is often our own adult perceptions that sow the seeds of contradiction and conflict. Will it not be better that the home and school act in coherence with a common approach and understanding?

Each child brings her unique experiences from home, making each a different individual. Home emphasizes the uniqueness and individuality of the child whereas school provides a common framework for socialization and acquisition of new knowledge and skills. There is a parent in every teacher and a teacher in every parent. The teacher can reach out to children only when the parent in her/him manifests itself. Parents become the first teachers in the child's life. Before starting school, it is the parents who provide him/her with a learning environment. Parents and teachers have to work together, complementing each other's role in order to provide the feeling of continuity, vital for the child's growth and development. Of course, it can never be identical. Nevertheless, the contradictions have to be minimized in the early part of the child's life.

6

Harmony at Home

Growing up in an environment of warm feelings and trust provides a sense of security and belongingness to young children. As they grow, they carry this sense beyond the confines of the family, to the outside world. Obviously, parents set the tone and pattern of behaviour at home. It is in childhood experiences that one finds the roots of an individual's basic ideas of right and wrong, basic emotional patterns, ability to enjoy and get along with people, sense of independence and self-reliance and attitude towards work and play. Parents are the primary models of emulation for children. However, it is not uncommon for parents as well as children to complain that they are not in harmony with one another. Many parents tend to complain that their children do not listen to them, are uncontrollable, argumentative and create perpetual tension at home. The story from the children is no different. They argue that their parents do not try to understand them; are indifferent to their feelings, perpetually nag them and are critical of whatever they do. How do we ensure a harmonious and warm environment at home right from the start, which children and parents can enjoy together?

Primary Responsibility lies with Parents

There is no standard approach for maintaining harmony at home. Most of the unpleasantness at home is temporary. Both parents and children have to take it as part of being human, giving space for venting their opinions and ideas.

However, it is important to take care that an unpleasant environment at home does not linger on for too long as this could adversely influence the growing child. Some broad principles may help parents in this regard.

Treat children as children and not as adults

Is it fair to expect adult behaviour from children when they have neither the mind nor the body of an adult? Try to recall your childhood days, and how you felt in situations similar to those that your child faces today. This will help you understand him/her better.

Do not expect your child to be a little lady or gentleman with manners and a sense of responsibility of an adult. Even though your first born is the oldest, he/she is still only a child. He/she has not lived long enough to learn the adult ways.

Respect the individuality of children

Treat them as unique individuals. They differ in their physical, socio-emotional and intellectual traits. Respect their likes and dislikes and their hopes and aspirations even if they are different from yours. Do not compare the child with other children of the family or neighborhood. If they do not come up to the standards that you have set for them, do not criticize them. And, even if they can, your fault finding may take away the natural urge in them to try and excel in what they do. Be a nurturing parent. Not sometimes, but always.

Allow them to express themselves

Talk freely with your children and let them talk freely with you as well. Approaching them with a constantly critical attitude will just put up a barrier between them and you, and get you nowhere.

Get to know your child's friends as you will get to know more about your own child from them, since these children have a powerful influence on the way your child thinks and acts.

Do not cross examine and do not demand that they tell you all things at all times. When your child comes to you with a problem, talk over the problem. It is the psychological moment to help him/her. If you put yourself on a pedestal, and expect them to look up to you as a demi-God, you will not get close to them. Talk to them as an equal and you will understand them better.

Parents can help their children and create harmony at home

Even during the early years, children need opportunities for playing creatively, and need to be engaged in meaningful work experiences so that they learn to share, to take turns, and to take care of things. Such experiences teach them self-reliance and independence on the one hand, and co-operation on the other.

They need experiences to explore, experiment and to exercise their imagination. Parents can help their children to develop such a behaviour pattern in a natural manner. For this, they have to demonstrate such behaviour themselves and work with their children.

Working together around the house encourages the feeling of family unity and oneness. There are many household chores that can be shared by everyone. Dusting, cleaning, putting things away, shopping, cooking, and gardening – these are some of the possibilities.

Children should have the choice and be allowed to do some of the things they enjoy doing. Disagreeable jobs should be shared by everyone, including the grownups. It is more fun when parents and children do things together and laugh and joke while doing them. This kind of working together helps children growing in a healthy manner both physically and emotionally as also appreciate the value of work.

Reading together, talking together, and watching television programmes together and perhaps, following them up

with a discussion, will go a long way in this direction. Other examples include trips to the museum, art gallery, zoo, airport, post office, watching a house being built, and going for nature walks. Talking and listening to each other is the heart of language development. It also builds in the child the desirable vocabulary that is critical for harmony at home. Your conversation with your child is as important as the actual work that you do together.

Mama, Do You Still Love Me?

Amala, a five-year-old girl, pushed her little sister. Her sister got hurt and Amala was rebuked by her mother. Her mother said, 'I will not talk to you, because you have become a bad girl.' After that Amala forgot about the rebuke but went on asking her mother, 'Will you never talk to me again?' She was really frightened that her mother may not speak to her at all.

Anant asks his mother repeatedly, 'Tell me Mama, if I do not get good marks in my final exam, will you still love me?'

Parents of Richa, an eight-year-old, are upset that she does not greet the guests. She was told that they would not take her out if she behaved like that again.

Are you confusing the child?

Amala's mother was clear in her mind that her rebuke will give a message to Amala that her act of pushing was bad and that she should correct her behaviour. But did Amala get the same message? She thought that her mother would not speak to her because 'she is a bad girl.'

At this stage, children find it difficult to differentiate or understand whether the rebuke from their parents is directed at the act, or at them. It is very important that we specify the reason for getting angry.

We could say, 'I did not like the way you pushed your sister. I am upset about your pushing and that is the reason I am angry with you.' It is alright to express your anger, but make sure that the child understands that the anger is directed at the action and not at her.

Children need unconditional love

Let us look at the cases of Anant and Richa. There is nothing wrong in expecting your child to do well in the examination or that she should be more social with guests. But Anant got the message that he would not be loved if he did not do well in the examination. He developed the fear of losing his mother's love. Richa's case is no different. It is normal to expect that your child socializes with your guests. But Richa may not be in a mood to talk to the guests, or she may want to do something else which she likes. She does not understand the relationship between being denied an outing and her behaviour with the guests. For Richa, (as much as for most children of that age) going out with parents is an expression of their love for her. She fears the risk of losing her parents' love.

In both cases, the parents acted out of concern and affection but the children internalized the message differently. They would like parents' love to be 'unconditional' and not linked to their daily behaviour. This is quite normal.

All children need constant reassurance from us of our love for them and that no conditions are attached. The challenge before parents is to make their children understand desirable behaviour while still letting them know that they are loved.

What helps children feel emotionally secure is the knowledge that their parents are there for them and will be on their side, no matter what they do. This does not entail that parents must always agree with them even when they are wrong. However, children need to know that their parents are supportive of them and value them.

Your love shapes your child's personality

Children who feel that they are loved unconditionally are eager to share their thoughts with you because of the closeness you share with them and because they know that they can count on you to keep on loving them.

You are someone special to them as no one else could be. They need to permanently share their moments of pleasure, even tiny secrets, with you and unhesitatingly seek your help in finding solutions to their problems.

A child may be told that he is loved but unless he feels that he is loved, he does not believe it. A young child looks for those small gestures of love from you by way of hugging or kissing or inviting him to sit in your lap. This physical demonstration of love though trivial for the adult, is important for the child as a means of reassurance.

A child, who feels loved, also develops greater self-confidence. As a result, he is more willing to take on challenges and become friends with others because he knows he is worthy of friendship. A child who does not feel secure in your love tends to become withdrawn, gets hurt easily and is likely to get angry very quickly.

Feeling of security is mutual

Just as the child may feel unloved, we may also sometimes feel that the child is not listening to us and we are losing him/her. Sometimes, we are afraid that by correcting the child, we will drive him/her away and therefore desist from pointing out mistakes to him/her. This, in the short run, may make us feel comfortable. But in the long run, the child is likely to feel neglected and consequently become emotionally insecure. Just as children worry that we may not love them, when we do not take time out to help them and correct their actions, we cannot help but develop the feeling that we too are losing our children's respect. It is important for parents and children to develop a mutual base of emotional security. An important part of this mutual bond of emotional security is the feeling of being respected. Though we feel quite sure of ourselves, as parents we need to always get the child's point of view before acting in matters that concern him or her, to understand the situation as it appears to the child. After all, the child has very limited experience and sees life from a physical and mental angle that is different from that of adults. The onus, therefore, is on the parents to create a climate of mutual respect and emotional security. Our children accept and love us for whatever we are. Let us also love our children for what they are, not for what they can become.

III. All Children Are Not the Same: Facilitating Their Development

As children grow from infancy to adolescence to adulthood, all of them pass through various stages of development. All cross similar milestones though the pace of change and development among them could be different. And, each child grows up to be a unique individual with a complex personality. As children grow, parents and teachers find some children unusually different from others, for instance, some have low attention span; some remain shy while some others are unduly aggressive. How does this happen?

There is no mystery to this. Children acquire their unique characteristics through interaction between the basic genetic disposition and a multitude of environmental factors. How should we as teachers and parents understand and help children develop into wholesome personalities capable of achieving their full potential? This is the subject of this chapter. Through illustrative cases of development problems, an attempt is made here to help parents and teachers on how these could be addressed. Should we be concerned about every angularity that we observe in our children? Probably not; many of these wear off as children move through different stages of development. It would of course be a matter of concern if these persisted.

This chapter discusses:

I. Understanding the Aggressive Child

II. Can We Increase the Attention Span of Children?

III. Helping Children Who are Shy

IV. Dealing with Temper Tantrums

V. How Do We Help Children with their Fears?

VI. Helping Children with their Emotions Through Play

VII. Dealing with Learning Disabilities: The Dyslexic Child

Understanding the Aggressive Child

A mother of a five-year-old child expressed her anxiety about her son becoming too aggressive. On probing, she said that he hits others and if things do not happen his way, he yells and screams. This is not unusual. Generally, children exhibit aggression by beating and bullying others, hitting, kicking, screaming and throwing things, pulling their own hair, or banging their heads. Through these actions, they hurt themselves, or hurt others.

What could be the reasons for such aggressive behaviour? The reasons can be classified into the following categories:

- o Physiological: Children may show an aggressive tendency when they are hungry, tired, or not feeling well. Lack of proper sleep and rest, or any physical discomfort can cause this kind of behaviour.
- o Socio-emotional: When they are not accepted and attended to, they feel insecure and ignored. Consequently, they show attention seeking behaviour by hitting and shouting at others.
- o Environmental: One of the reasons for aggressive behaviour lies in the environment prevalent at home, parents' attitude towards the child, parental favouritism, too strict or permissive handling and comparison between siblings. When children are constantly nagged, compared, and favoured over the other, they get upset and angry.

- Influence of Television: When they view television and other video films which show violence, they indirectly conclude that it is a socially accepted behaviour and try to imitate it.

How we can help our children to channelize their aggression?

- We need to engage them in different activities like reading, painting, music and different outdoor games, where they can give vent to their pent-up energy. Also, this gives them a sense of achievement.
- Many children throw tantrums when their demands are not fulfilled. One can divert their attention, if children are very small. If they are old enough and able to comprehend, telling them in simple language that such behaviour is not acceptable may help.
- We have to reason out with them that each of their demands cannot be fulfilled.
- We have to ignore them when they are at the height of their temper. We may leave them alone.
- It is important that we do not provide a model of aggressive behaviour to the child.

Can We Increase the Attention Span of Children?

Very often we hear comments such as 'I did so much but he does not pay attention,' or 'I switch off the T.V. when he does his home work but nothing works,' or 'I do not know how to make him concentrate on anything.'

These need not be the comments of a habitually complaining parent. Indeed, some children are unable to focus their attention on any task for more than a few minutes. What could be the reasons for the short attention span of children? It is a complex combination of genetic, biological and socio-emotional factors that affect the attention span of children. As parents, we cannot do much about the biological make up, but we can influence the socio-emotional environment in which they grow and mature. Attention span can be strengthened by modifying our own behaviour and by providing a socially and emotionally conducive environment. Following are some tips to increase the attention span of your child:

What you can do to increase the child's attention span

- Listen to your child patiently. Your patience helps him/her to develop a sense of security and in turn, it helps him/her to relax and focus attention.
- Be sure you pay attention to your child when he/she is talking to you. This is important if you want your child to learn to pay better attention to your words as well.

- Involve yourself in your child's activity. Your involvement will help your child to engage in the task longer than he/ she would have done alone.
- Encourage the efforts of your child. Your encouraging words help him/her to concentrate and continue the activity for a longer period of time. Your silence when your child concentrates on a task is likely to be perceived as lack of interest from you.
- Follow a consistent schedule for your child. This helps the child to know what to anticipate or what is going to happen next.
- Avoid nagging your child for not attending to something when you want him/her to.
- Give activities which are not only interesting but also challenging. This helps children to sustain their attention. Too easy or too difficult tasks may lead to frustration and boredom.
- Help your child to develop interest in a variety of activities like painting, music, dance, sports. If your child can do these activities for a longer period of time, it leads to habit formation. The habit gets transferred to other areas of activity and in the course of time, he/ she can concentrate even on studies.
- Encourage your child to play and work with other children. Participation in group activities and observation of others while they work influences your child's behaviour too.
- Be sensitive to your child's physical needs like hunger, thirst before he/she settles down to do any work. Even mild sickness such as cough and cold can cause him/her to be inattentive.

Helping Children Who Are Very Shy

Many parents often worry about their children being too quiet and shy. The common complaint is that their child does not talk freely or mix with other children. He/she prefers to spend time either reading, or playing alone. Should this be a real cause for concern? Why do children behave like this? And, when should we as parents and teachers start worrying about it?

Very often, adults tend to consider a quiet child as a well-behaved child and this may reinforce the child's behaviour. There is nothing wrong if some children are a little shy by nature. They may be shy simply because of a new environment; and they may take little longer than others to adjust to new people and places. But excessive shyness or persistent signs of withdrawal are a cause for worry.

Very quiet children may be feeling a number of emotions. They may be deeply unhappy or emotionally depressed which is outwardly indicated by their shyness or withdrawal. One has to find out their reasons for being shy or withdrawn. Children who are shy could also be feeling neglected at home. They may be quiet because they are afraid of adults who have been unkind to them and feel the threat of being ridiculed. It could also be that the child is being constantly compared and nagged. In many such cases, the authoritarian environment at home leads to lowering of self-esteem, which in turn makes the children withdrawn.

Children acquire several adjustment mechanisms in such conditions. You must have observed some children trying to cope with it by sucking their thumb or fingers, or holding on to their old blankets in times of stress or insecurity. Slightly older children go through phases of being very interested in their own body parts and find pleasure and comfort in playing with themselves.

How do we help them?

- They require a trusting, friendly environment to come out of their shell. One needs to build a feeling of trust by talking to them without any pressure on them to respond, involving them in different play activities.
- Your affection and kind gestures will help them to build confidence. This may involve spending time together reading out stories, playing games, listening to music, or simply listening to them, which helps in the expression of emotions.
- They look for consistency of behaviour in adults in caring for them so that trust can be built. Your sharp criticism and harsh words may damage their esteem and drive them into their shell.
- Depending on the age of the child, they should be encouraged to express their feelings through words, painting and other creative means of expression or through make believe play.
- If you still find that the child remains seriously disturbed then it is advisable to take the help of the counsellor in the school.
- Shyness or withdrawn behaviour is invariably a temporary state of mind, which can be rectified through care and concern.

4

Dealing with Temper Tantrums

It is not unusual to find small children throwing tantrums at the most unexpected occasions. Of course, some children do so more often than others. A wide range of events can spark off their outburst of temper. For instance, if the child is playing with a toy car and the car does not function properly, the child gets annoyed and throws the car. Or, you are preparing to go out for a family picnic and it starts suddenly to rain heavily. The child feels frustrated and begins to scream and cry. You find it totally unreasonable since it was not anyone's making. As children grow older, however, they are able to reason out and such behaviour begins to naturally disappear.

There can be many reasons why children may not outgrow frequent tantrums. For example, when the child was young, the parents may have given in to her wishes at the first sign of temper, which may have even surprised the child. It is not unusual for parents to do so in order to avoid an unseemly spectacle in public. For the child, however, it makes life so confusing and unpredictable that tantrums become more an expression of distress than temper itself. The child acquires the behaviour pattern as a means of communication, never having experienced that there are other ways of getting her point across. Handling a child's tantrums need patience and willingness to see the world from the child's standpoint. We as adults also need to be honest, to reflect on how much our feelings of pride or embarrassment at the time affect the way we handle the situation.

How to deal with children's tantrums?

One can often recognize patterns of behaviour in the child leading to an unseemly situation of screaming and crying. If we recognize the patterns, it is possible to distract the child from getting into that state. However, if the child too frequently gets into tantrums, it is sensible for the adults to leave the place quietly, so that there is no audience. One can also deal with the situation more positively. For instance, an older child might be encouraged to express her feelings through words and be helped to understand the situation once the scene is over.

Quite often, the problem is located in the child sensing that the adult is undecided and can be influenced. For example, whether or not the child can continue watching television, even after announcing that she should stop viewing it. The value of setting definite limits and being consistent can be of great value in dealing with children. Wavering between 'yes' and 'no' provides an opportunity for the child to influence the adult's decision through temper tantrums. For young children a firm 'no' is sufficient.

However, definite prohibitions have to be accompanied by willingness from adults also to think in a calm moment, about whether they are fighting a battle over issues that are not really important. It is possible to be drawn into a confrontation solely on the grounds of 'he has got to learn to listen to elders.' This may sound quite reasonable to you but the small child may fail to capture the reason behind your rigid posture.

Once a child has gone into a tantrum, she is beyond comfort, or reason. Calming words from an adult may have an effect slowly but it is the emotional tone of what is being said that calms, not the words themselves. The child needs to be safely contained – in some cases physically prevented from hurting herself or others.

Some children may be able to shout and act out the tantrum in a corner without being restrained. As the child emerges from the tantrum, she needs comfort from adults. In such situations, adults need to remain calm and refrain from reacting in anger and adding to the dramatics. Basically, if a child sees that she is gaining some benefit from tantrums, she will learn that these are useful to her and the tantrums will increase, rather than decrease.

Tantrums can sometimes become a more serious physical problem. Some children learn to hold their breath in a tantrum and their faces may actually turn blue or purple. This can be a very frightening experience for adults. In this situation, the best course for adults is to remain calm and not make desperate attempts to try to force the child to breath. Reason out with the child in a calm manner later on. Becoming desperate and yielding to the child only reinforces the physical response of the child.

Children who seem to be really testing parents' limits and setting off power struggles with them, may respond well to being given the opportunity to assume more mature and responsible roles. Try treating them in a mature fashion and you may find a dramatic shift in their emotional behaviour.

5

How Do We Help Children with Their Fears?

As children explore the outside world, they discover more things to fear. Unfamiliar people and places easily frighten children. They may acquire fear on the basis of earlier experiences. Minu screams at the very sight of a dog. This is because a dog had bitten her. Another common fear among children is the fear of darkness. Some of the fears about ghosts and monsters emerge as children develop their imagination. The nature of children's fears change as they grow older. They learn to overcome them with their capacity to reason out. These fears need to be handled gently and with compassion, otherwise they may turn into phobia causing psychological problems in their emotional life. If a child is frightened of something then we need to find the reasons for it. There is no point in trying to dismiss this as something they all have to grow out of.

Some fears are clearly sensible and protective. If a child has a fear crossing the road, there is reason to be cautious. Other fears are less easily explained because they do not seem to have reasonable cause. Why should anyone be afraid of a spider or a worm?

Such reactions are easier to understand if we recognize the role of cognitive processes in producing fearful responses. We fear not what will harm us but what we think will harm us. We interpret an event in our past experience, our present understanding, and the total situation. It is on this basis that we infer the event being either harmless or dangerous. The same stimulus – spider – might cause reactions ranging from amusement to interest and to fright in people of different ages, or with differing experiences.

How do we help children overcome their fears?

- Make sure that you create a safe environment for the child. You are there to help whenever the child requires. Like the fear of darkness, children also sometimes need reassurance about vague fears such as thieves, or things under the bed. For some children, fears turn into phobias, which can disrupt their lives. Children's feelings do sometimes emerge through their fantasy play. This may provide some clues as to how the fear has developed and also provide a context for talking to the child.
- Adults have to be very patient in building trust and creating a secure environment for children.
- Respect and understanding should always be accorded to children who are afraid of an object or event. Making fun of fears or shaming them in front of others does not help them to cope effectively with this emotion.
- Realize that children will outgrow fears. Some fears may take longer than others to overcome. They may require patient listening and exhibiting empathy and understanding.
- Familiarize yourself with the fears that children experience at different ages.

- Allow children to become accustomed to fears gradually. Try to understand fear in relation to the child's overall personality.
- Accept what children say. Give them a chance to talk about what makes them uneasy, following which you may be able to reassure them.

Helping Children with Their Emotions through Play

All of us observe our children acting out their feelings through play. They boss over their dolls and teddies – in the same way as they feel they are controlled by adults. Through the doctor-patient game, or while playing the role of mother, father or teacher, children often voice their fears, frustrations distress, and anger and also express their happiness and joy. The monologues and dialogues during their play may help us to understand their inner world, what they think and how they feel.

The traditional notion that very young children are always happy and stress-free is not fully justified. Children also face different kinds of stressful situations but they are unable to express their feelings through words as adults would probably do. Their medium of expression differs. They often reveal their complex emotions and inner conflicts through play.

Ritu had met with a car accident. She played out the incident again and again with her toy cars, until the memory did not haunt her anymore.

Five-year-old Rohit, who is often embarrassed and upset about bed wetting, expressed his feeling while putting his teddy to bed.

Rani, who is upset with the birth of her little brother, always talked about throwing him out of the window when she played alone with her dolls.

What do the above cases tell us? Ritu is playing out the car accident to overcome her fear of accidents, while Rohit and Rani are trying to deal with their inner conflicts through play.

Parents who listen to and sensitively involve themselves can observe their child's concern – expressed through play – about events at home, fears about other children, or thoughts about a particular experience. Such observations offer them opportunities to help their child deal with her/ his emotional stress and inner conflicts. Further, this would also help in resolving conflicts arising out of misunderstanding events and improving patterns of communication with children.

How do we help children deal with their emotions?

- We need to accept that children have strong feelings and are sensitive to subtle messages. It is important for us to see from the children's point of view – in terms of their feelings, experiences, and levels of understanding. This often needs honesty from adults to admit that their feelings are colouring their perspective and that there are other ways of seeing the events.
- We need to listen to their stories and tales. It is important to be patient when they play doctor, mother, father, and teacher, and not force our interest on them. Instead, we should try to enter into their activities.

Of course, it is a good idea to help them solve their problems without imposing on them, and equally important to follow their own interests and suggestions.

- We have to make a genuine effort to respond to a child's feelings, reactions, and problems as one individual to another.

- We should provide children opportunities by creating a play corner for them and encourage them to indulge in play acting. This would help them to clarify and master their emotions. It will also be an opportunity for them to vent out their feelings and develop a sense of well-being.

To conclude, children's play provides unique opportunities for parents and teachers to understand as well as shape their emotions. The kind of play they choose, the way they play it out, the words and stories they build into their play – each of these is shaped by the environment in which they live and, at the same time, presents a window to their evolving personality and emotional make up.

Dealing with Learning Disabilities: The Dyslexic Child

Anant is a seven-year-old boy. He is generally bright. But he seems to have problems differentiating certain sounds and words. He confuses 'saw' for 'was' or 'buck' for 'duck'. Further, he finds it difficult to repeat sequences of numbers or months of the year in proper order.

Anuradha, the mother of an eight-year-old daughter, Rima, is perplexed that her daughter can identify lyrics of all popular songs, can play a musical instrument with ease, takes interest in sports but forgets simple rules of grammar, avoids doing mathematics, and takes too long to complete her homework.

Children like Anant and Rima are obviously experiencing learning difficulties in school subjects. It is natural for their parents to be puzzled as to why their children are unable to cope with the demands of the school curriculum when they seem to be comfortable in every other way. Are these children lazy as very often their parents tend to characterize them, or are they dull as their teachers seem to suggest? Teachers find it difficult to deal with such children as they do not find any obvious reason for their lack of progress. It is unfortunate that sometimes they blame the child or the parents for not paying adequate attention to school learning. But this only increases the already existing tension and pressures for everyone involved.

Who are these children? Do they have a learning disability? Probably, they do. But learning disabilities refers to a broad spectrum of conditions that affect the learning capabilities of children.

The cases quoted here seem to be of 'dyslexia'. However, it is necessary to carefully study the learning behaviour of the child with respect to certain basic symptoms before concluding whether he/she is dyslexic. How do we recognize the symptoms of dyslexia? In a broad sense, a child with dyslexia may have difficulty in one or more of the following areas: (a) Reading comprehension, (b) Listening comprehension, (c) Writing expression, (d) Oral expression, (e) Mathematical computation, (f) Mathematical reasoning.

Usually, you will find that,

- This is an intelligent child who does not perform well at school.
- This is the child who reads words backwards: ' on' for ' no', 'saw' for 'was', 'God' for 'dog'.
- This child puts letters in the wrong order, reading 'felt' as 'left', 'act' as 'cat', 'reserve' as 'reverse', 'expect' as 'except'.
- This is the child who cannot picture things in his/her mind, who cannot visualize or remember what he/she sees.
- This is a quiet child who bothers nobody in the classroom but does not learn.
- This is the child who can add and multiply but not subtract or divide; who can do maths mentally but cannot write it down.

- The child is most often lost in space – cannot visualize spaces; gets lost in distinguishing between up-down, left-right, above-below, top-bottom, in-out.

It is hard for parents to accept the fact that they have a child with a learning disability. They are unable to understand why their perfectly normal looking intelligent child does not learn or behave as other children of her/his age do. Parents go through different stages in recognizing that their child has a learning disability. Usually they start with a denial response to any suggestion that their child has a learning problem and most often, end up with acceptance and either despair or hope.

Can a child with learning disability succeed in the adult world?

Most of the dyslexic children grow up to be normal achievers. Many children never excel in reading, they are poor in spellings but they still become successful in business, mechanical fields, architecture, the arts and many other occupations. Some become exceptionally creative and imaginative problem solvers. Some have become doctors, scientists, politicians, and generals.

There is a need to create awareness among professionals, teachers, as well as parents to the problems of the 'dyslexic child'. They need to identify these children early in their life. If by Class II, a child is really not doing well, and if a good deal of what has been taught earlier cannot be recognized, it may be worthwhile at this point for parents to seek professional help.

They need to find a diagnostic center and have the child tested. If there is no diagnostic center, parents should try to find a psychologist whose specialty is psychological testing and has adequate knowledge of learning disabilities.

Guidelines for Parents

- o Early identification and acceptance of the problem of learning disability by parents can help the child.
- o Try to motivate your child without pressuring him/her. Do not point out spelling mistakes all the time, instead spend time if you can, in playing educational games, praise smallest achievements and encourage him/her to build on his/her strengths.
- o Do not compare your child's performance with others. Do not lose your temper if your child is not progressing at the pace you want. Overcoming the problems associated with dyslexia can take a long time. A lot of patience and hard work on everyone's part is required. It is essential that your child feels that you are on her/his side. This gives her/him a sense of security which is important for learning.
- o Whenever you or your child get frustrated while working together on reading and writing, leave practicing for a while, till the tensions have eased.
- o Keep in touch with the teachers. There has to be clear communication between you and the school regarding different aspects of the development of your child so that problems can be dealt with jointly and more effectively.

IV. Building Creative Spaces for Children

Children left unconstrained have a natural inclination to explore their environment irrespective of their age. As they explore, they not only become curious but also get engaged uniquely and creatively with various aspects of their surroundings – physical world, animal world and human beings around. At the same time, the modern world tends to cramp children's activities into a straight jacket, almost permanently pushing their daily life into one of routine mediocrity. Obviously, this should be a matter of concern for all parents and teachers. This chapter discusses the possibilities of enriching the life of the children through a variety of mediums like art, music, drama, and storytelling. The main purpose is to help parents find ways and means of bringing out the creative energy in their children. It further discusses how parents and teachers could build creative spaces for children and be creative themselves in their approach and thinking; how to accommodate children's perspective in their dealings without being critical and without imposing any stereotypes.

I. Art in Child's Life: Reaching Out to the Creator of the Art

II. Rhythm and Music in Your Child's Life

III. Child's Play: Drama in Real Life

IV. Do you Remember Stories that You have Loved Hearing as a Child? Tell These to Your Children.

V. Your Child is also Creative

VI. Nature is a Part of the Young Child's World

Art in Child's Life: Reaching Out to the Creator of the Art

Four-year-old Minu is engrossed in drawing. Her mother gets upset

'My daughter just scribbles and doodles,' she comments.

'Why don't you make a nice puppy instead of just scribbling?'

Naman, a five-year-old boy, when asked to draw his family, drew a big version of himself in the centre and his Papa and Mama to his left and right.

The teacher is trying to fix Salma's drawing because she has drawn flowers and leaves in the sky and coloured them yellow.

Let us try to understand what these little creations convey to us? Are we able to reach out and understand the human being behind the art, or are we only reacting to the output? When a child creates something, it is a natural process of expression. It is not just a drawing but a reflection of the inner world of the child – her world of emotions, imagery of life spaces around and the untapped creative energy within. The scribble is a record of the child's physical movements, coordinated with her/his thinking and feeling which springs from her/his experiences.

Most children begin to doodle between the ages of two and four and continue even after they have begun to draw real objects. Doodling is an important activity that all children indulge in. It is one of the first means of symbolic expression. It is thus important that we do not discourage this, holding the wrong notion that doodling or scribbling is baby-ish.

All children follow a relatively similar sequence. They begin with scribbling and progress through more systematic and increasingly complex forms and ideas. Since this growth is interwoven with the child's total intellectual and emotional existence, it should not be viewed in isolation as simply a series of activities intended to enable the child to pass time happily. At this stage, the child uses a lot of symbols to express feelings and thoughts. For instance, a small dot in the picture may represent the pet toy that the child plays with, or a little brother or sister.

Very often, we are quick to pass judgment on a child's creation and try to fix the drawing. If a child colours leaves blue, we consider this to be wrong and tell her/him how it ought to be. Through such comments as 'draw a nice puppy' or 'you can't have leaves in the sky', we indirectly dictate to the child 'what to draw and what not to'.

By not approving her drawing as it is, the child is likely to get the message that we do not approve her ideas, her creation, and perhaps her as well. Instead, listening to the child and talking about her drawing would help her to feel secure and reassured that we accept her. Of course, you can convey how differently you would have done it. This kind of conceptual freedom will help her to be not only creative but also more self-confident. Further, it also gives an opportunity to the child to recognize that there is not always only one right way of thinking and representing objects and events in life. Accepting others' views and sharing with others is also a part of learning.

So what should parents and teachers do?

- o Encourage children to draw. At the initial stage let them use crayons rather than pencils.

- o Allow them to experiment with colours freely. Give them space and freedom to draw and paint what they like.
- o Children like to draw on the walls and floors because it gives them a sense of unrestricted freedom. Naturally, we do not want our walls to be soiled. You could possibly paste old newspapers/calendars at a lower level where children can reach and feel comfortable to draw. Learn to be more tolerant of the 'mess' that your child makes.
- o Allow them to talk about what they have drawn. Listen carefully to the stories they have to tell about their own creations. They convey many things to you and help you to understand your child better.

- It is fascinating to observe the changes that emerge in your child's drawing, as she grows. You will find changes in terms of coordination, proportion, form, lines, colours, detailing of the objects, and clarity of various concepts. It is a gradual process of change, corresponding to the physical, emotional and intellectual development of the child.

- If you can bring out the child in yourself, perhaps you can enjoy your child's creation better. Reassure your child that you accept her ideas and imagination. This will boost her self-image and develop confidence in her. Who knows, maybe your child is a little artist in the making!!

The drawings of children invariably reflect a rich physical environment, the sun, the moon, trees, birds, and animals. They not only appreciate the beautiful things of nature but also attempt to capture them in their creations. Children observe and understand the environment in relation to themselves and other people. You can easily see that children always view themselves as part of nature and not as a separate entity. What a wonderful message for us!!

2

Rhythm and Music in Your Child's Life

'A three and half year old Damu moved rhythmically to the tune his father played on the drum.' 'Lily clapped when songs were being sung to her.'

It is not surprising to find children responding to rhythm, music and movement, spontaneously. Rhythm is an integral part of a child's life. Children have learnt this from the very beginning of life, perhaps in the womb of the mother. They begin their life experiencing rhythmic movements, as life itself is based on the rhythms of the heart beat, pulse and breathing. Everything in nature has a rhythm. The sun rises and then it sets. Our bodies breathe in and breathe out. We wake up and then sleep. All repetitive behaviour, routines and rituals provide a sense of rhythm to life. All children need this rhythm and ritual. There is a time to play, a time to eat and a time to rest. This gives them security. The security of regular routines and rhythm helps them to become responsible, self-directed and confident individuals.

Music itself involves both rhythm and sound. The first rhythmic movements of young children are stimulated by sounds. It is a common sight to see children dance to the tune of music, stop crying when they are rocked, and feel comforted by the soft sounds of lullabies. You must have observed children clapping to a beat then moving their legs and feet. This is because the rhythmic development of young children follows a sequence. First, their arms and hands and later, their legs and feet move to a rhythmic beat. Gradually, they learn to move according to soft and loud sounds and try to explore the world of sound. They use their own voice to experiment with the language of sound, as a means of communication.

They are fascinated by the various sounds in the environment – the sounds of birds, animals, the pitter patter of rain, rustling of leaves and the blowing of wind. They learn to identify and discriminate the sounds in the environment. Before they can talk, they are happy to sit on an adult's lap and listen to nursery rhymes being sung. They love to listen and sing rhymes and songs. They enjoy tunes, repetitive words and rhythm in the songs. They will sing the song which they have heard and they will experiment with sounds and make their own tunes.

These acts of observation, imitation, exploration and experimentation help them to master the language. Songs rich in emotional content and feelings appeal to children. There are various songs and rhymes especially for children covering a wide range of themes from daily routines, family, birds, animals, sun, moon, stars, transport, festivals and stories. The rhymes and songs not only provide fun but also help in promoting children's language learning and clarification of concepts. Children love to dramatize and perform simple actions while singing a song. It gives them a sense of excitement.

Movement is one of the earliest forms of communication that children explore and learn because it allows for the expression of ideas and imagination without words. Music and movement help in exploration of time, space and energy. Developmentally, children explore the environment through movement and learn about the body and how it can move. Movement fosters physical muscular development in children. It also helps in channelizing their emotions.

Learning through movements can provide excitement and allows creativity in the integration of various themes.

So what should parents and teachers do?

- o Encourage children to listen to the sounds of nature. Ask them to close their eyes and listen to the sounds and talk about it. Children enjoy identifying sounds and reproducing them. It is a good exercise for developing listening skills.
- o Allow children to move to the sound of music. Children love rhythmic movements. Change the rhythm from fast to slow and from loud to soft. This is helpful in identifying children who are not able to differentiate fast-slow and high-low sounds.
- o Play a game to imitate the movements of different animals and birds. For example, hops like a rabbit, jump like a monkey, fly like a swan, etc. This will help them to discover and refine their inventive movements and be creative in their expression.
- o Children enjoy listening to music and making music. It is not necessary that adults need to be good singers. What matters is their interest and enthusiasm when listening to music or singing with children.
- o Singing will often arise spontaneously when children are working and this can be used as an opportunity to introduce new songs.
- o Create music corners where children can experiment with rhythm and pitch and explore the world of sound. They should experience the joy of making music.

- Children are usually interested in watching someone playing an instrument. If it is possible, let children listen to instrumental music or live orchestra performances.
- Introduce them to different musical instruments and demonstrate what each one sounds like and how musical beats can be produced. Drums come in all sizes and shapes. Let them try beating the drums to any rhythm.
- Allow them to listen to music. This will help them to appreciate the tune and the rhythm of music.
- Record what your child sings. Let her/him listen to the recorded song. Children enjoy listening to their own voices.

Music and movement should be made into fun for young children, with no burden of expectations. It should be for their enjoyment and not for performance or perfection at this stage. This should be a pleasurable experience that helps them discover and understand music and movement and their appeal.

3

Child's Play: Drama in Real Life!

It is fascinating to observe children play. A three and a half year old child playing with a doll, talking to the doll about what happened in school as if the doll were a living being is a normal response. Playing out is natural for all children. They try to reproduce situations they experience in real life. One finds a clear sequence of 'pretend play' in young children. By age two, children can pretend and often play with imaginary objects. You may find your child playing alone with toys as if they are real people or animals. It is a common sight to see children imagining a stick as an aeroplane, wooden blocks as kitchen sets, and a teddy bear as a lion. It comes very naturally to them to use symbols, imagine substitute figures and create new characters which are not there and derive happiness and joy from this. Pretend play almost always makes use of creative imagination. Representing reality in a symbolic manner is an important step in mental development. Children live in a fantasy world, knowing very well that they are only pretending. It gives them a sense of security and self-confidence if we, as adults, appreciate their imagination and become their playmates.

Readiness to play with other children is part of the developing self as well as a step in the sequence of socialisation. This is also an indication of the emerging self-identity. Those children who have a strong sense of identity interact well with others.

Very often we see them play the role of the mother or of the father when they play ghar ghar (house), teacher, doctor, police and various other roles that they find in their social world. In enacting these roles, they are learning to see the world from others' point of view. This is an important life skill. Acting like their mother or father helps them to build new relationships.

Children are always seen experimenting in their play and trying to find out about themselves and the world around them, especially people they know. Their ability to understand other people is dependent, to a great extent, on their own self-perception. Through play acting, they begin to understand their own feelings and behaviour in relation to others. As they grow older, their dramatization becomes more elaborate and complex. In fact, play acts as an integrative force by providing opportunities for children to clarify who they are and understand their relationship with others.

How does pretend play help children?

Enacting and dramatizing is a natural medium of expression for children. How often we have heard children doing a running commentary while playing alone with their play material, or dialogue with their playmates while assuming different roles. This helps us to understand their inner world – what they think and how they feel. The monologues and dialogues sharpen their language and communication skills. Often, they rehearse the use of new words and expand their vocabulary. It gives them an opportunity to express themselves, coordinating their body movements with the words, as also the accompanying emotions.

- Through dramatic play, children develop a sense of independence, gain self-confidence and understand the behaviour of other people. They become more observant of the world around them.
- The playful use of imagination helps them to develop a sense of self-identity. In the process of becoming someone else, they become more of themselves. This gives them the opportunity to practice interpersonal skills. It also helps them look at their own capabilities and limitations in a realistic manner.
- Play provides opportunities to clarify and master emotions. It gives them the opportunity to vent their feelings, which in turn gives them a sense of well-being.
- It provides scope for the development of imagination and creativity in children. They create their own stories. They develop their own dialogues. They become directors and actors.
- Play acting can also help clarify concepts through actual use. For instance, children love to play the shopping game – buying and selling. This helps them to learn the concepts of measurement and volume, know the prices of different articles, and communicate with others.

How do we build this creative space for our children?

- By creating a play corner for them and providing them with a variety of materials like dolls, toys, utensils, toy-cars, puppets, wooden blocks, empty boxes and mirrors. The articles should be within their reach and safe to play with.

- By encouraging them to play, by listening to what they say while playing and by being a part of their play as and when they require us to do so.
- By telling them stories and encouraging them to make their own dialogues and enacting them. This would provide very rich inputs for language learning. By playing games with them in which they imagine and act like different animals, birds, and people. This would nurture their creative impulse and give them tremendous self-confidence as they grow.

Do You Remember Stories that You Loved Hearing as a Child? Tell These to Your Children

When asked to narrate the most memorable experience of her childhood, Mona talks about listening to stories told by her mother. She vividly remembers how she looked forward to sitting in her mother's lap and listening to stories of kings and queens or the wonderful animal stories. Very often she would imagine herself as one of the characters, forget her own identity and be transported to another world for a while. She loved those stories where she used to repeat the sounds tabadak tabadak (sound of a galloping horse), and play act with her mother. She would ask her mother endless questions. She cherishes this memory even today. She says, 'As a teacher and a mother, I would like to provide the same experience to my children.'

The memories of warmth and joy of early life still live with Mona. Perhaps, this is true with most of us. We all grew up listening to stories about the good old days that appealed to us very much. While listening to stories, children learn more than just about the characters and plots in the stories; they learn about life, their family and their place in the world. They learn to relate events of their everyday life with what they hear in the story. Children learn the values of courage, honesty and loyalty, played out in stories, and are motivated to live up to these values. The story books also possess the magical quality of taking the reader from one moment in time to another, or from one location to another.

What kind of story books do we need to select for our children?

There are certain things that we need to keep in mind in selecting story books. As we all know, children like books which are illustrative, attractive and colourful with big print. This helps them sustain their interest. We need to provide age and stage appropriate story books. For instance, young children of 3 to 5 years like to listen to stories of animals, birds, trees, sun, stars, moon etc., in a nutshell, everything around their immediate world. They appreciate repetition and rhythm in the stories.

As their world expands, by around 6 to 8 years of age, they like to listen to stories about people, fairy tales, folk tales, and mythological themes. At this stage, they tend to indulge in daydreaming. The stories transport them into the world of imagination. The stories with 'Once upon a time there was... They lived happily ever after' attract them as they feel secure being part of such a world. For many children, the characters in the story become an integral part of their own life.

At the next stage of development, that is pre-adolescence and adolescence stage, they love to read biographies, stories of adventure, and mystery, and also start taking interest in stories of romance. At this stage they are searching for their own identity. Stories of great personalities inspire them to emulate the ideals they represent. This is also the stage for hero worship. It is very important that we provide the right kind of reading material which helps in shaping their personalities.

Although we have talked about age and stage appropriate reading material, there are individual differences. Some children prefer to read more of adventure, while some may like to read fairy tales and still others may prefer stories of animals. We should keep in mind the varying interests of different children. It is very important that we do not impose our stereotypes on them. The language should be simple and graded so that they do not lose interest in the story.

Making story reading time a memorable experience for the child

Many a times, we leave children alone with books and we expect that they would read and enjoy them. But merely providing books do not help in inculcating the habit of reading. We need to sit together and read out books to them or read with them.

It is worthwhile to have a special time for storytelling. Reading together also establishes an emotional bond between parents and children.

We need to discuss with them their views about the characters of the story – the reasons for liking or not liking a particular character. We must encourage them to imagine themselves as those characters. By doing this, we help them to develop their thinking and problem solving abilities.

Children are always ready to act out, or play act parts of their favourite stories. Give an appropriate voice to each character and read out their dialogues in that voice. Allow them to express themselves freely when assuming the role of the character that they are playing and share the character's emotions and feelings.

Your Child is also Creative!

All parents want their children to be creative. This is natural. But are you really developing creativity in your child? Read the following incidents.

Akhil's teacher narrated to him an interesting short story. After a couple of days, the teacher asked Akhil to narrate the story in the class. Akhil was a good communicator. He narrated the story with a lot of enthusiasm and actions. Other children in the class were really thrilled with the story. But the teacher was unhappy. Akhil's mistake was that he had added his own bit to the story and ended it in an altogether different way from the original.

Was Akhil wrong or was he being original and creative?

Minu's mother encouraged her daughter to paint. She bought several books with outline figures so that Minu could fill them with colours. After a few days Minu's mother found that figures in only one book were filled with colour. The remaining had not been touched at all. Instead, there were several imperfect drawing of animals and other figures. Minu was scolded by her mother for wasting paper with those unattractive drawings instead of systematically learning the art of painting through colour books.

Was Minu wasting paper or was she creating something?

When children freely draw or express themselves in any form, they are giving us a sample of something unique and distinctive about them. These are the means that children use to express their thoughts and feelings about the world around them. By nature, the child is original.

Each child has something unique to express and has a special way of expressing it. In all forms of expression, whether it is drawing or telling a story, children follow their own rules and not those of the adults. In contrast, we as adults expect them to follow the beaten path. We, thereby, not only perpetuate stereotypes but also negate the development of original thinking and creativity. We generally expect our children to follow the pattern that is shown to them.

What stimulates a young child towards creative action? Everything that happens to the child is exciting. Each new person, animal, object or nature form is stimulating to them. Many of their expressions, therefore, are their attempts to translate the stimulating experience into art forms using a variety of material like paper, cardboard, wood, clay, and paint. All children wish to draw, paint, or model just as long as they have fun, creating. Children express themselves creatively on all that they see, feel and think. Most of their creative ideas come from the wide world of first hand experiences. Children would like to consider that the result of their expression in its entirety belongs to them.

They like to look at the finished products just as you and I did when we were young. The product may not be perfect in the eyes of others but the stimulating effect of the action of producing something original is in itself a valuable experience.

Many parents feel comfortable when children draw, paint, or write stories which are realistic. Will the emphasis on fantasy and creative expression reduce the child's understanding of the real world? The world of make believe is as vivid to the child as the real world. The young child does not see a rigid distinction between the real world and the world of imagination. Fairies, toys that walk and talk, princesses and flowers that dance together really exist for them. It is easy for them to picture fantastic stories, dreams, feelings, and joys. We, as parents, could help by being enthusiastic about the translation of imaginative stories into objects of the child's own creation.

How do we promote creativity in children?

- To begin with, we need to believe that each child is a potential creator, thinker, and experimenter. For this, we need to create a learning environment where they are not afraid of asking questions and exploring their surroundings. Their exploratory questions are not to be branded as dumb ones.
- We have to provide a supportive role where we give our honest and constructive feedback to them rather than negative criticisms.
- Provide them with such activities where they have to see themselves in unusual circumstances. For instance, exercises like brain storming, simulation, mind mapping which take them beyond conventional thinking would prove highly stimulating.
- Help them to recognize their own potential and encourage them without imposing your standards and ideas.
- Allow the child to display his or her own work at home, irrespective of how good or bad they are in your view.

- As parents and teachers, we need to reflect and think about how to alter our practices and perceptions in order to promote creativity in our children.
- Children should be encouraged to work at their own pace. Putting pressure on them and making them worried about how others will judge what they are doing will kill their creativity.
- Do not destroy the inner joy of creating something original by excessive use of rewards such as prizes, toys, etc.
- Too many instructions in their day to day life of 'what to do' and 'what not to do' could confuse children as they may get the feeling that being original is not appreciated and any exploration is a waste of time.

6

Nature is a Part of the Young Child's World

Five-year-old Shahid was fascinated by the procession of ants passing through the corridor. He stood there and watched them going in a line. He followed them. He was curious to find out where they were going.

Swati is delighted to see how a pigeon is feeding her little ones and teaching them how to fly. She observed them growing from being little ones into full grown pigeons. If she learns to observe and admire this, she will have learned one of the greatest of all lessons in nature. This is a part of life that is common for all living creatures.

Kabir has always shown interest looking at the sky and finding out different constellation of stars and their position. This nine-year-old boy reads to find out the details of movements and positions of stars.

While there is no end to what can be learned about nature, the process starts with learning to look and observe. Children feel close to birds, animals and flowers for they themselves feel a part of nature. In fact, these are the lessons that children find easier to learn. As you pay more attention to the nature that lies around you, you will find that your own understanding steadily increases, helping you to share the world of nature that your child feels for. Once you start showing the living world to your child, you will be surprised to see how much of it is a part of your own everyday experience.

We all want for our children a world filled with beauty and wonder and delight. This wonder and delight exists all around us. It lies in nature. Children are born curious and are interested in understanding the world that they live in. We need to guide their enquiring minds about the beautiful world of nature. We must remember that one question leads to another, and finding the answers is a game without an end.

How do we help them develop an interest in nature?

Children love playing with water and sand. Give them an opportunity to do this. This not only helps them to be in harmony with the rhythm of nature but also to develop skills of exploration.

Help them to nurture plants. You do not require a big garden for this, even a small plant in your balcony or the little space in front of your home will do. Caring for plants helps children to discover that plants grow. They learn to build up a sense of respect for nature and the environment.

Encourage them to listen to the sounds of birds, animals, and insects and help them to observe their living and eating habits.

Children should be encouraged to observe natural phenomena, for instance, sunrise and sunset, or the changing seasons. This again helps them to understand and appreciate the rhythm of nature.

Go out for a nature walk. Children acquire enormous amounts of knowledge from interacting with nature. They learn concepts of colour, size and shape by observing things around them. Facts of nature are so well integrated with life that children enjoy acquiring knowledge from nature.

Allow them to collect things whenever they go out for a nature walk – objects like twigs, leaves, feathers and nests. Encourage them to speak about the things they have collected and help them to write about the things they see and hear. It is these experiences that they carry throughout their lives which make the world a vivid place for them.

The power of wonder and curiosity in influencing the lives of children as they grow is truly amazing. It deepens their wisdom. The more they know, the more they find it interesting. This sense of boundless mystery comes to all of us when we gaze at the stars. Teach your children to look up and wonder. Show them the constellations in the clear night sky. The more they learn about the world around them, the more reverence they will have for it. Remember, reverence for life and nature is the very foundation for building the character of children.

V. The Learning Child

'Learning' is the core objective which parents aspire to fulfill by sending their children to school. However, learning is not confined just to school and the classroom. It also happens at home, outside the home, on the playground, and anywhere, throughout life. Yet, school occupies a significant place as it equips the children particularly in their early life with the skills of reading, writing, and arithmetic. These skills form the instruments for acquiring new knowledge and additional capabilities. But the young child in the early years of schooling is still growing and transitioning through various stages of development. The need, therefore, is to harmonize learning (acquiring skills of reading, writing and arithmetic) with the process of growth and development of each child. The goal of harmonizing learning with development in young children, guided by teachers and parents, is the subject of this chapter. The objective is to help parents and teachers to understand the underlying processes so that learning tasks given to children are appropriate to their age and stage of development. This chapter also deals with the issue of providing a stimulating environment at home and at school that facilitates learning without burdening the child.

I Developing Listening Skills in Children

II Children Learning to Speak

III How Do We Make Reading Fun for Children?

IV How Do We Help Children Acquire Writing?

V What is Difficult about Learning Arithmetic?

VI Science is a Part of Everyday Life

Developing Listening Skills in Children

Ferzina, is a seven-year-old girl. Her teacher complains, 'She is regular in attending the classes but does not seem to listen to what I teach.' Likewise, Raghu's mother complains about her six-year-old son, 'I tell Raghu to bring something specific from the room but he brings something else. This keeps on happening.' Probably, Ferzina and Raghu are physically present but not listening to what is being said – listening to the teaching taking place in the classroom or to the instructions given by the mother. Why is a child all ears to the story being told by her grandmother but inattentive to what the mother or the teachers are saying? To listen means to take notice of another person's communication. Active listening means showing someone that you understand what they are saying by nodding your head, smiling and repeating or reflecting back. Obviously, the degree of listening depends on their interest. The difference between a good listener and a non-listener is not just the hearing ability but something more complex. We all know how important it is to be a good listener, not just for learning, but for life, in general. So how do we encourage our children to be good listeners?

To begin with, let us try to understand different levels of listening. This may help us to understand the significance of the different levels of involvement and concentration. We can differentiate at least six levels:

- o Hearing sounds of words but not reacting to the ideas expressed.

- o Intermittent listening: paying attention on and off
- o Partial listening: following the discussion only well enough to find an opportunity to express one's own ideas
- o Listening passively with little observable response
- o Listening critically: questioning everything?
- o Appreciative and creative listening with genuine mental and emotional responses

A good listener not only thinks with the speaker, but s/he flexibly anticipates the speaker's direction of thought; objectively evaluates the ideas presented by the speaker and mentally views the facts represented by the speaker.

How do we develop listening skills in children?

It is very important that we as adults demonstrate to children the art of listening. Children have many things to share, their experiences in the school, the playground and all that happened during the day. They look forward to sharing their experiences with us.

If we listen to them, they get the message that what they say is important. This gives them a sense of confidence. They also learn to listen when you talk to them. But for this, we have to be active listeners, appreciating their responses with understanding and emotions. It is not enough to listen half-heartedly or be passive listeners, as many parents do. Listening with full attention is needed not only for developing mutual respect but in becoming good listeners. We can design a number of activities that help in the development of listening skills in children, without becoming overbearing on them.

- Children love to listen to stories. Story telling is a powerful medium for developing their listening skills. It is after storytelling; a variety of activities can be conducted like illustrating the story, retelling the story, and dramatization.

- Try to produce your own recording of sounds which occur every day in the environment or ensure that the sounds that the children are expected to identify are both familiar and easily distinguishable.

- In a small group, tell the children that you are going to say words of which some rhyme. Demonstrate what a rhyme is since they may not necessarily know. Ask them to indicate when they hear two words that rhyme.

- Take children for a listening walk, may be in a garden. Ask them to listen carefully for a short period of time and then tell you the sounds that they have heard.

- Play music for children and ask them to listen very carefully. When the music stops, ask them how the music made them feel.

- Play a small selection of musical instruments. Hide the instruments behind the screen and play them again, except for one, then ask them to identify which one you left out.

2

Children Learning to Speak

Two-year-old Ranu repeats almost every word that her mother speaks. Is it unusual? Not really! In fact, it is very common for children to echo words that they hear. Perhaps, they are practicing speaking. When they begin to speak, they try to imitate the speech sounds of those around them. As they listen and practice, their vocal organs become more adept at making different sounds. Usually, children with normal speech and hearing abilities are able to produce most of the sounds that adults use.

Young children aged three to five, are just at the stage where their speech begins to develop quite rapidly. From simple two word sentences that they vocalized earlier, they are now able to expand their sentences and express their thoughts through longer sentences. Young children learn their language by interacting with objects, both living and non-living, in their environment, and acquire the words that these objects are represented by. The more the child interacts with objects, the more words the child will be able to learn. Just as they play with blocks, toys, and each other, children also play with words. They make up nonsensical syllables, repeat word sounds, mix up words, say words backwards, make up chants, and repeat rhyming words. They infer the meanings of words as they hear them in real life situations.

At first, each word is used only in one way and with only one meaning but gradually they discover that they can call, direct, demand, point out, play with and ask things by means of intonations in pronouncing the word.

You must have observed children indulging in monologues in which they manipulate sounds, patterns, and meanings of words. With older children, sound play contains more meaningful words, consonants, and blends. Children often repeat words in a nonsensical way – ham, bam, and wham. Pattern play is a common form of play that involves manipulating the structure of the language. The child begins with a pattern and then substitutes a new word each time s/he says it. For instance, 'Bobby go out', 'Mummy go out', 'and Daddy go out'...

Using words and sounds in an unusual manner is part of the process of acquiring mastery in language skills, particularly in the spoken language. Children learn to use the correct form on their own as they grow and observe the adults using the words in different contexts.

They often try out and practice unusual sounds and syntax with their peers. Sometimes children, who have problems speaking words, are able to sing words. Adult approval is critical for them to experiment with sounds and words and through this, master the art of speaking.

How do we provide a stimulating environment to develop their spoken language?

Adults can make a real difference to children's language development by making conversations an enjoyable experience for them. Very often, adult speech is in the form of instructions instead of engaging children in a conversation that is fun and enjoyable to them. Our conversation with children, whether brief or long, can have a significant impact on their spoken language, if it takes account of their language ability, both in terms of speech and understanding. Spend time talking to children in a normal fashion. Talk about anything that interests them. You do not always have to be the instructor who is teaching the names of vegetables, colours, fruits, and vehicles.

Giving opportunities to children to speak and converse with you is very important. We often ask questions that require straight 'yes' or 'no' answers from them – Have you seen my spectacles? Do you want to eat? We can, however, also ask open-ended questions which offer opportunities for them to speak. Similarly, when your child comes to you with a drawing, do not simply say it is good. Instead, ask her to describe what she has drawn. Allow her to carry on the conversation as long as it holds her interest.

Children love to listen to your childhood stories especially the funny and silly things that you did when you were a child. This not only helps them in relating to you but also enables them to make a link between the past and the present while speaking.

Telling a child about something is more than just giving information. Conversations have detailed descriptive qualities which influence the speaking ability of the child.

Children, in the early years of their development, as their language evolves, enjoy making up stories that involve the imaginative use of language. Speech as imagination, may take place in a variety of fantasy contexts. For instance, fantasy conversation may be about animals in the garden or it could be about events that have never taken place or about fairies and demons.

Children often enact such situations among their peer group with full intonation of voice and actions. Encourage them in such acts. Encouraging spontaneous imaginative play is one of the best means to motivate and promote language growth in them. Such occasions require the child to produce original dialogue in words and forms that are socially acceptable. In fact, peer group conversation amongst children often takes place in a dramatic form.

Children also learn to speak correctly by listening to others and comparing their own speech with what they have heard. Therefore, encourage children to learn to listen to others. When they read or narrate stories, record them. Play these tapes and allow them to listen to their own voice. Reading books or telling stories aloud helps them in their spoken language. Basically, our role is to be available when they want to play with words, objects or toys.

3

How Do We Make Reading Fun for Children?

Reading begins when a child is two and a half years old, and starts listening to stories. Listening to stories is the first step in the sequence of learning to read. The next step is to read out stories together. Reading aloud develops a child's ability to read alone. This happens naturally to many children who sit on their parent's lap to listen and watch the finger of their parent or teacher move across the page, pointing to the words, as they are read.

Very often we see small children spending endless amount of time looking at picture books. All children can read wordless books in any language. They can 'read' most picture books from the pictures alone. They are always happy looking at books about animals, birds, flowers, trains, airplanes, ships, stars or the moon.

Reading is not a mechanical skill. It is more than simply recognising letters in words, or grouping sounds into words. Children need to understand groups of words and derive meaning from reading. They must learn to read not letter by letter, or word by word but in terms of thought units – whole phrases and sentences.

The emphasis has to be on the meanings of the words that make sense to them. Using whole words brings into focus the meaning of words in a contextual manner. It is important to present words with meanings that are concrete and something that children are aware of, rather than giving sound and spelling correspondences which are abstract in nature.

How can parents prepare children for learning to read?

This can be done by reading aloud stories that children want to hear and in the process, pointing out to them the title of the book, names of the characters, animals and objects.

It is essential to talk to them about the book and about the story, as it unfolds while reading it. Help them observe where the reading begins and follow with the finger as it points to the lines that are being read. Gradually, they will learn that print proceeds from top to bottom and left to right.

Point out labels on containers in the kitchen, signboards on shops and roads, street names and hoardings. This provides a gradual induction into the world of print. By this, children will learn to recognise certain familiar words like corn flakes, biscuit, tooth paste, tea and street names, without going through the routine of alphabet learning.

Keep books handy. Choose books that your children like to read. Help them to look at books as their friends. They will gradually learn to accept books as a necessary and natural part of everyday living.

Remember that children's attitudes towards reading often depend on their parents' attitudes and behaviour. Children, who observe that their parents are in the habit of seeking information and enjoyment from books, tend to enjoy reading as though it is natural to them as well.

Ask the child what he/she has drawn and write out the labels and titles for them. This would convey to the child that words can be seen in the context of the meaning they have imputed in the drawing. Thus, illustrating with printed words begins to be associated with children's thoughts and ideas. Read out to them what has been written. This will help them to understand that what has been spoken, can also be written.

A child's mental development influences learning to read. Some children mature faster than others, some are slower to develop mentally. Their social and emotional development may also determine their learning. Children, who are ready to read, usually show mental, emotional and social maturity.

Allow children to read for both the meaning and pleasure. Start the reading process with aspects close to children's own experiences and those which relate to their evolving needs and interests.

Through books at home and in the library, make reading material available on different topics. Increase the difficulty level gradually so as to foster growth in their reading skills. Provide varied experiences that will give them the background to pursue meaningful reading, later in their lives.

Not all children learn to read at the same time and pace. We need to recognise individual differences. As we do not expect all children to learn to walk, or to talk at exactly the same age, so it is with reading. We should not try to force them into reading when they are not ready, as this may lead to tension and anxiety and permanent reading problems.

How Can We Help Children Acquire Writing Abilities?

Quite early in their life, most children enjoy making squiggles on paper. This is their first natural attempt to write. All children who squiggle seem to think that writing is something that can be read, and they sometimes pretend to read these as mock writing. This is the first attempt in the natural acquisition of writing. Once their squiggles have become horizontal lines instead of circular markings, this is an indication that they have begun to understand that writing is something different from drawing. If you observe their first squiggles, they do not resemble letters at all. Children, in fact, try to copy only the broad, general features of the writing system; that it is arranged in rows across a page which consists of a series of loops, long strokes and connected lines that are repeated. Gradually, they learn to differentiate the finer features of the system, the letters.

Writing is an activity which integrates many different processes – physical, linguistic, cognitive, social and affective, in different ways. It involves eye-hand co-ordination. During writing, movements in fingers, wrists, arms and shoulders as also movements of the eyes for monitoring writing have to be coordinated. The fact is that learning to write is largely an act of discovery. Children need to practice writing just as they do for speaking.

This does not mean that we should sit down with the preschool child and formally teach her to write. Instead, we should fill her environment with examples of the written language. Teachers serve as models by doing a great deal of writing and reading in the presence of children, and provide with the tools and encouragement to attempt writing on their own.

If you are wondering how and from where they acquire this knowledge of written language so early in life, look around you. Children are surrounded by written material – in newspapers and magazines, in television advertising, on the labels of food products, in letters in the mail, in the stories read to them, on signboards on stores, on stickers on cars, etc. The printed word is everywhere. Some families encourage their children to print their own name at an early age, and family members take time out to write out the stories that their children make up. They are further encouraged by family members, who themselves are engaged in writing or reading.

How do we promote creative writing?

A good start to begin with the written language is with children's own names. Encourage them to write their name on their personal possessions. Help them to identify their own name tags. Children can write messages in pretend scribbling. You can write the real words below their mock writing.

For free exploration, children should be given unlined sheets. You will find them writing all over the page without inhibitions. Lined paper may inhibit this free form exploration of how writing works. Some children need better eye hand coordination before they engage in writing. Finger painting on paper gives the children practice doing linear mock writing with their fingers. You need to praise them for their efforts in all the writing that they do, just as you praise them for their art.

Let children play with alphabet blocks and magnetic letters at first. Have alphabet games books and magnetic letters available to them and let them choose what they want to play with. Read out an appropriate alphabet book but do not teach formally. Or, if you have a computer, pick out the first letter from someone's name, then spell the entire name.

Some children write reverse letters or write upside down. This visual discrimination problem may have to do with their perceptual skills. With practice and maturity these problems resolve themselves unless the child has a learning disability. The best way is to fill the environment with words, letters, and opportunities to write as well as to support and encourage children's own attempts at writing.

Read aloud many stories. This will help children in the development of the imagination and ability to use words creatively.

It is not only materials from stories which children interweave with their own imaginative writing; they also sometimes use the raw material from their own lives in their stories.

Children love to keep a book of their own in which they may draw and record their thoughts, and which they claim as belonging to them – 'This is my book and this is my drawing, or writing. It is a constant reminder to us that the starting point with young children should be their homes, their families.

Very often, the question of spelling and punctuation arises when there is an adult's discussion on children's writing. If children's spelling is corrected at too early a stage, it may curb the creativity of the child. They may become so engrossed in spellings that their work will become unimaginative and stereotyped, confined to using words they can spell.

Children enjoy writing stories and many of their first attempts will be recalling stories which they have been told, or which they have read. They should be provided with a rich and varied selection of stories. Not only will they develop a vivid and well selected vocabulary but they will also learn to associate books with pleasurable experiences.

5

What is Difficult about Learning Arithmetic?

Children's experience in the world of mathematics begins almost at the time that they are born. The sensory experiences that they gain through the movements of their body leave them with the appreciation of space. Before they come to school, they already experienced a wealth of mathematical situations. 'I am a small girl', 'Oh! She is only a little baby' are illustrations of a mathematical vocabulary which children have learned from their experiences of talking and listening, and through everyday happenings. They are also familiar with, and have some understanding of, such terms as long, short, big, little faster, high, and low.

It is a misconception that children acquire the notion of number and other mathematical concepts only from teaching. On the contrary and to a remarkable degree, they develop these concepts independently and spontaneously. When adults try to impose mathematical concepts on children prematurely, learning is merely verbal; appropriate understanding of them comes only with their mental growth.

This can be easily shown by a simple experiment. A child of five or six may readily be taught by her parents to name the numbers from one to ten. If ten stones are laid in a row, she can count them correctly. But if stones are rearranged in a more complex pattern or piled up, she no longer can count them with consistent accuracy. Although the child knows the names of the numbers, she has not yet grasped the essential idea underlying the number, that is, the number of objects in a group remains the same, and is conserved, no matter how the objects are shuffled or arranged.

What do one and two make? This is unfamiliar to most preschool children. Such a use of language occurs very rarely in conversations between four year olds and their parents at home. When number words such as one and two do occur, they are almost invariably referred to objects like one spoon, two spoons and so on. Questions like 'what do one and two make' represent the formal code of arithmetic. They do not make reference to any particular object or entity. They are context-free. This is a source of difficulty for children.

This observation provides a new perspective on the difficulties confronting young children. The problem is that they are encountering a novel code, and trying to find a link between the formal language of arithmetic and their existing number knowledge. The question then is, whether young children can create these links for themselves, or whether they need to be helped. The answer seems to lie in the fact that most preschool children do not translate formal code questions on their own.

How do we help them to understand mathematical concepts?

Children should be helped to understand the mathematical principles which govern their everyday life. If we let mathematics remain an integral part of their life, they will not have the fear of being unable to cope with a superimposed set of rules and conventions that they have to learn at a later stage.

Children who are confident of their ability to deal with simple number situations will soon realise the necessity to know more. Their willingness and cooperation in the learning process develop because their needs are being satisfied.

Most young children show a lively interest in numbers – in bus numbers, the numbers of houses, etc. Very often they are so obsessed with numbers that they count everything within sight. At first, this counting is done with the help of adults but as soon as children can count on their own they do not take help.

Buying and selling is a game that children enjoy from an early age. In playing this, they are experimenting with mathematical language, a language they tend to acquire without understanding. They need to handle money, to play with it, to shop with it. A shop can provide many opportunities to master the understanding of balances and weights. It should be stocked with objects of different shapes and weights.

Children's readiness and the ability to accept the formal logical procedure of mathematics is dependent upon their development and the experiences they have at home before coming to school. Their understanding of numbers develops slowly. They count, based on the idea of a one to one correspondence, that one object corresponds to one.

Once children reach ages four and five, they become ready for experiences that involve recognising and naming the properties of numbers. They need vast experience in counting manipulative objects before they begin to combine and separate sets. The ability to understand the processes involved in combining and separating sets is similar to what is needed for mastering addition, multiplication, subtraction and division. The basis of this understanding can be provided if children are given concrete manipulative objects with which they can experiment. At the primary stage they should be given ample experiences in combining sets (addition, separating sets, subtraction and combining equal sets (multiplication).

As young children begin to manipulate objects, they should be encouraged to use verbal representations for each object. As the verbal symbols begin to be understood, children are anxious to read and write numerals. Reading and writing numerals should not be stressed upon until the child has had many manipulative and counting experiences.

Science is a Part of Children's Everyday Life

Science is not just a subject. It is an approach and an attitude towards understanding ourselves and the world around us. If this is the meaning we use then there is a scientist hidden in every child. How do we bring out and nurture this scientist in the child? A prerequisite for nurturing such an attitude is the need for freedom – freedom to explore, freedom to express, freedom to think, freedom to act and freedom to create. But do we do this in real life? What do we do as parents and teachers? As adults, how do we deal with our children? We need to reflect on this.

How do we make science a part of their everyday life?

- Water is an ideal medium for simple science. A basic concept which can be explored with water is floating and sinking. This can lead to a series of games. For example, to find out things that float and those that sink, introduce children to plenty of objects from simple everyday life. Ask them to divide the objects into two groups – floaters and sinkers. Ask them, what do all the floaters have in common? Why do some objects sink? Although floating and sinking are difficult concepts, children may usually conclude that heavy things sink and light things float.

  But, as soon they find that this does not fully explain what they actually observe, it raises new questions and curiosity in their minds. This is science.

- Empty containers of different shapes and sizes can also help them to learn the idea of volume. Ask children to choose the container which they think can hold the most or least water. There are endless variations one can think of while playing with empty vessels and water, all of which are really simple science. They may not arrive at a definition of volume but will begin to explore the meanings of shape, size and volume.
- Cooking is an applied science. When different ingredients are mixed together such as flour, water, etc. they change into something else. Sometimes, you can change the nature of objects and then change it back. For example, if you put water in the freezer it turns into ice. Take it out of the freezer and it will turn back into water.
- The garden is another place which serves as an enjoyable environment to learn science. Let children learn about gardening. Children love to water plants. Ask them why they water plants and you will see a whole lot of science emerging. Children should be encouraged to look for wildlife in the garden for different colours, shapes and forms of plants, insects, etc.

  Looking at insects fascinates young children. It can be fun observing and following a butterfly's movement from one flower to the other or watching ants going in a line. Children will have endless questions in mind as to how the butterfly flies without falling, what it does sitting on flowers, why ants go together in a line, and so on. Encouraging and developing observation skills are a very important part of science learning.
- The changes in the weather are also an endless source of fascination for young children. The starting point to study the weather could be by looking at the sky and trying to describe what they see in the sky. A game

that can be played with children is about weather words. They may be asked to think of words that have something to do with the weather. Young children can be encouraged to keep a simple weather chart by drawing pictures of the sun, clouds, rain, etc. One can also make a simple rain gauge with a wide necked container and funnel. Comparing bottles of rainwater collected at different times in a week gives much the same understanding about the week's rainfall.

- Children's fascination of the sky often extends beyond sunset. Commonly asked questions include, where does the sun go at night? It is possible to keep a moon chart in much the same way you can keep a weather chart. The only difference is that it helps if the moon chart lasts for at least four weeks. Older children can make their own drawings on the chart, showing the moon's shape. After four weeks, a pattern should emerge, showing how the moon gets bigger until it reaches full moon, and then gets smaller until it disappears and then gets bigger again. The stars form patterns in the sky which children should be able to recognize.
- Keep children's science simple. Encourage their natural curiosity. When you think about it, you will find that you know a lot about science in general terms even if you thought that you knew nothing and the subject was beyond you. Make the activities fun and you will be laying strong foundations for understanding the complex concepts of science. If children do not want to know at a point of time, leave it. 'Free exploration' is at the heart of science learning and children's interest in exploring their natural surroundings begins from early childhood. Science is not something that children learn only at a later stage when studying it as a formal subject.

VI. Securing the Child's World

Every child from birth to becoming an independent adult has to go through a long period of infancy, childhood, and adolescence stretching over nearly two decades. The extent of security the individual feels during the process of growing in early childhood is likely to shape the personality of the individual significantly in later years. How do we provide a secure environment for our children? This is the concern of every parent and teacher. Children as we know are often unaware of the physical and emotional threats lurking to hit them. For instance, it is not uncommon to hear about children being abused physically and harassed mentally. Sometimes, people who are expected to protect the child may themselves be the cause of the threats and the ensuing damage to the child's personality. It is, therefore, important to raise awareness among teachers, parents and other care providers on the ways and means of securing the child's world in the school, at home and outside of the home so that the child is protected from harm that may affect her/him both physically and emotionally. This is the main focus of this chapter.

2. Protecting the Child from Abuse
3. Breaking the Barrier of Silence
4. On TV Viewing: To Watch or Not To Watch
5. Helping Children in Homes with Separated/Divorced Parents

Protecting the Child from Abuse

Eight-year-old Manju began her school life as a bubbly, outgoing child, who easily made friends with teachers and other children. Suddenly, she became very quiet and started sitting alone. Even during the recess she sat alone. Her smile disappeared. The drastic change in her behaviour was noticed by the teacher who called Manju and spent some time talking to her. During this interaction it was revealed that she had been abused by her own uncle. Manju's teacher counseled her with great care and sensitivity and helped Manju regain her confidence and slowly become how she originally was.

Lakshmi, a young parent did not bother too much initially when her five-year-old son complained of pain in his groin. When the pain persisted she took him to the doctor. To her horror, she came to know that her son had been abused by the boy who was looking after him.

These stories about Manju and Lakshmi's son point to a much larger concern. We come across reports of several children like them too who have been subjected to physical and sexual abuse. Studies have shown that mostly it is people closest and known to children who abuse them. Abusers can come from any walk of life, including, well-respected people whom you can never imagine could indulge in such an activity. The culprit in many cases may be a relative, a neighbour, your own friend, a care taker, or even a teacher or someone in school or outside home who knows the child.

In the normal course, we do not find this to be an alarming problem. However, in cases where this does happen, it can be permanently damaging to the child's personality.

Thus, care and caution by parents is critical. If at all it happens, one has to know how to handle such events and their after effects. Children disclose such experiences in a variety of ways when they are physically abused. Very often, we come to know through their behaviour as in the case of Manju. The kinds of statements they make may lead us to suspect abuse. However, often parents neglect to see a change in their child's attitude or reprimand the child for not performing well or worse still remain in a state of denial even when they have suspected something unusual.

Parents have to be alert at two levels: (1) when you sense the possibility of abuse in a particular setting caution your child to stay alert; but do not show undue anxiety. It is not immoral to talk to your child on these aspects; communicate as early as possible to the child through age-appropriate language, on keeping himself/herself safe. Better safe than sorry! (2) Be alert to any changes you see in your child's temperament or performance, ask your child casually of the associations in school, outside home, sometimes, even in the home, especially if frequented by relatives or parents' friends when parents are not around or the tutor who gives tuitions, etc. But do not jump to conclusions on your child's changed temperament and reprimand the child for his/her poor performance, lack of attention, etc. Instead, talk and probe in a gentle and trustful manner.

How should children be helped?

- ***Listen patiently***

  Listen to the child without questioning in front of others. Make sure that the child feels comfortable and does not feel guilty or ashamed to tell you about what all happened. In order to minimize the child's anxiety, do not project your own anxiety on to the child. It is important to speak quietly.

- ***Create a relaxed environment***

  Allow the child to speak voluntarily. Do not force the child to disclose far more than what he/she wants to say. Allow the child to tell the story without interruption. Many children feel anxious and apprehensive that people around them may not believe them. Try and use language appropriate to their developmental level. Accept their version of sexual terms.

- ***Allow the child to express feelings***

  Assure the child that he/she is not alone. Abuse happens to many children and that adults want to help them. Impress upon them that talking and telling about the abuse to adults is the right thing to do. Children who have been sexually abused may develop feelings of guilt, shame, and fear. We need to convey to them that these feelings are normal and will wear off in course of time.

- ***Reassure the child that the abuse is not his/her fault.***

  Emphasize that it is the adult who is supposed to act responsibly and therefore should feel guilty. Tell your child that he/she has done nothing wrong, either by participating, or by talking about it.

Protect children from abuse by being sensitive to their needs, and by making yourself a trustworthy and sensitive person to whom they can disclose such information. Children often hesitate to reveal physical abuse to their parents for the fear that they may harm the family through such testimony. Let this not be so. Assure the child to feel comfortable and to freely express himself/herself, and assure him/her that their talking about their abuse will, in no way, harm the family.

2

Breaking the Barrier of Silence

There are a number of occasions when we feel the need to shield our young children from unpleasant realities around them, given their tender age. In this process, sometimes, some of us make up stories or give misleading answers to our children. Still others relieved that their children ask no questions, tell them nothing. They assume that if their children ask no questions the happenings around them have no effect upon them. Often, we seem to mistake their silence for peace of mind. Of course, no parent wants to burden a child with details of illness, or mishap in the family which he/she cannot understand. But a simple explanation, suited to his or her age and understanding could help remove the confusion and worries in the mind of the child. Many a time, evasive answers and partial information intensify the child's fears. The child clearly perceives that there is something wrong but feels that it is not right to talk about it. The real problem lies here, in the attitude and behaviour of adults and their perception of the unpleasant realities that threaten children. Instead of the child being allowed to bring his fears, fantasies and confusions out into the open, so that they can be discussed, the child feels repressed. Being quiet about these fears, fantasies and confusions does not mean that these feelings disappear. They continue to be part of the child's unresolved burden of emotional life.

Let us try to understand what happens to children when we create a barrier of silence by trying to avoid talking to them about unpleasant realities.

Raman's father suffered a mild heart attack and was admitted in the hospital for a couple of weeks. His mother told him that his father was fine and will be home soon. Raman had many things to ask her but she never gave him a chance to find out any further details. Raman felt responsible for his father's illness since he felt he was harassing his father. He even believed that he was to blame for the heart attack. He carried this burden and a feeling of guilt along with it.

Not all children react in the same way to family crises and difficulties. But when parents listen carefully to what children say, they can very often find out what is on their minds and deal with what may be bothering them. We need to give them opportunities to break their silence and let their worries and conflicts come out, so that they can be dealt with as they arise and in a timely manner.

Take another case, one of parental discord at home and its impact on children who silently bear the brunt. Let us try to see how the parents' can minimize the children's confusion in such a situation.

Anand and Arti were undergoing a lot of tension at home. They decided to get separated. Keeping in mind the best interest of their children – eight-year-old Aniya and six-year-old Aman – they told their children only as much as they could. They told them in clear terms, 'Both of us love you but the two of us are not happy together. It will be better for mummy and daddy to separate. It does not mean that we stop being your mother and father, or stop taking care of you."

Of course, such explanations are not going to fully prevent the children from undergoing emotional trauma, but, it will definitely help them to lessen their confusion. The experience of being abused or separation or divorce of parents is a disturbing experience for any child as it affects his/her emotional development. Whether or not it will do serious harm to him/her depends very largely on how the whole matter is handled. In case of a separation or divorce, a child needs to feel that although his/her parents are not able to live together, they respect each other and love him/her deeply.

Separation, divorce or even continued misunderstandings and fights among the parents are the most difficult things to talk about to children. Many parents – having decided that separating or not communicating with each other even while living together – put off telling their children about the situation. Often, they feel that it may emotionally disturb their children so it should be avoided as long as possible. They do not realize that evasion may damage the child's mind more than the shock of hearing the truth.

> *Silviya was a six-year-old girl when her grandfather died. Her mother could not bring herself to talk about it, or answer Silviya's questions. Her mother thought that it was best to tell her simply that he was old. God loved him so much that he has taken him away. But Silviya was still troubled that there was something strange about it. She could not sleep properly. She had a number of questions in her mind but was afraid of asking them, or felt guilty that by asking such questions she would increase her mother's grief.*

Many parents find it very difficult to talk about death. But by keeping quiet, they only increase the child's confusion and fears. Normally, very young children neither need nor want detailed explanations. However, if death does occur in the family, silence or evasion does not keep them from realizing that something very unpleasant has happened. They also get affected by it.

Parents should give children an opportunity to share their feelings and help them to learn that grief, just as much as happiness, is a feeling one can show and will experience. The important thing is to give children opportunities to ask questions and to express their thoughts and feelings. Without words, fears cannot be talked about. Parents should certainly not go overboard and tell a child more than he can take but the confusion or the traumatic emotions that result due to silence can be far more painful than the truth.

Children feel much more threatened by the unknown, by their fears and confusions than they are by facts, no matter how unpleasant they are. Parents need to break the barriers of silence that surround many things, including, death, divorce, illness, sexual abuse, and allow children to talk about their fears and confusions. With the knowledge that they can share their innermost thoughts that are troubling them and can talk to their parents, teachers or care providers without fear of any untoward consequences or reprimand, they develop an enormous sense of security which keeps them well guarded, protected and feeling loved.

On Television Viewing: To Watch or Not To Watch

Unheard voices of our children

Let us listen to these conversations of children. What do they convey to us?

Akshay: *You know, yesterday I watched the WWF show. I never miss that slot. But my Mom and Dad hate it. Which is your favourite programme on T.V.?*

Manu: *Oh, I love watching the Cartoon Network. Of course, my mother also complains that I spend too much time on it. What about you Akshay?*

Akshay: *You know in my home the T.V. is on all the time so I watch whatever interests me.*

Rani: *I like to surf channels and find out about different programmes. I do this most of the time except during dinner when my father is very particular about watching the news.*

Mini: *I find my mother watching serials but I am not allowed to watch and often I argue with her to let me watch programmes that I would like to.*

This is not the story of just these children. In fact, many children are hooked to the television, spending a lot of time watching anything and everything. In the process there is less interaction among family members and with the outside environment as well. T.V. plays a significant role in influencing relationships, attitudes, desires, priorities and values. Before meaningful dialogue between the parents and the children breaks down, we need to find ways of stopping the invasion of T.V. in our personal lives. There are many simple things that we can do as adults to promote media literacy among our children.

Do not make T.V. watching a whole day activity

Many people use the T.V. throughout the day. Mrs. Sharma was watching a T.V. serial while ironing her clothes. But she did not allow her five-year-old daughter to watch T.V. while doing her homework. Instead she asked her to go and study in her room. Children do not appreciate our double standards. Placing restrictions on T.V. viewing is seen as unjust by them. Children will follow the same pattern of behaviour as we do and it will be difficult to change the habit. If you are watching T.V., you should watch it for the programme. Avoid making television the backdrop for other activities.

Avoid using T.V. at dinner time

This is the time for being together. This is an opportunity for family discussions, sharing, exchanging notes and remaining connected with each other. Children look forward to narrating their experiences of the day during dinner as they can generally get the whole family together. It is a precious opportunity for them to share their ideas, views and opinions on different issues. It also makes them feel heard and attended to by their parents. Watching television at dinner distances parents from children and vice versa. Worst of all, parents deny themselves and their children the opportunity to build good communication within the family.

Do not surf channels

It is not only children like Rani but adults also often indulge in channel surfing, setting a model for our children to follow. Gradually, channel surfing becomes a pastime. It is necessary to impress upon children that viewing a programme on T.V., be it a cartoon, WWF or any game show, has to be more focused. If you are interested in a particular programme, you may find out the schedule from authentic sources and view it. Otherwise, engage in some other alternative activities like playing indoor or outdoor games, or reading with your children. Channel surfing can ultimately lead to a moronic addiction.

Remain in touch with what your child watches on T.V.

It is very important to know what kind of programmes your child is interested in. Of course, they may not interest you but, it will help you in understanding the kind of programmes your child likes and the kind of influences they could be prone to.

It is important for parents to familiarize themselves with the contents of the weekly T.V. guide to ensure purposeful viewing for their children. Young children have difficulty distinguishing the 'real' events and characters from 'unreal' ones. They are unable to perceive and understand the real worth of some T.V. programmes. Parents could help them to understand this by commenting on the programmes. Some televisions come with a child lock which parents could use to block any programmes that they consider age-inappropriate.

Ensure the whole family watches T.V. together

It is important that the whole family view some programmes together. In this situation, you could encourage your children to talk about the programme, their reasons for liking or not liking the programme. Children will gain better understanding and knowledge when parents explain the events they view. Further, parents should critique and voice their opinion about the programme and encourage their children to do the same. This will help them to discriminate worthwhile from worthless programmes as also develop their critical thinking and questioning abilities apart from perhaps developing an interest if not passion, in the subject of the programme that the parents would like them to watch. Avoid as far as possible to let children watch programmes on their own without engaging them in a discussion on the programme.

You could use T.V. as an instrument of learning

T.V. often has a wide range of educative programmes. It would be a good idea for the teacher to tell children in advance to watch a particular programme. This may be followed by a variety of activities like holding debates, discussions, quizzes, and planning a project. Talk about the characters. Do they appear like real life characters? Help them to think about what they see on T.V. Give them the opportunity to talk about their likes and dislikes. We must help them to think about the quality of the programme, the characters, the presentation and the message.

Watch out for T.V.'s invasion in your life

Remember that you, not the television, are the master. If you do not like what is on, then do not watch it. You have the opportunity to select what to watch and what not to watch. T.V. viewing is one of several activities that we do in our daily life. It is for us to set the right priorities for watching T.V., among all these activities. Parents need to realize that the guidelines for a good T.V. diet are similar to those of good nutrition. How much T.V. should children watch? What kinds of programmes are appropriate? These questions should be carefully considered. For physical growth and development of the child, we are committed to providing nutritious food. Similarly, ensuring a good T.V. diet for the children's social and intellectual development is equally important.

4

Helping Children in Homes with Separated/Divorced Parents

A young mother who is herself undergoing the trauma of separation worries about her child. The child thinks that 'Papa no more lives with them because he (the child) has become naughty and does not listen to him (the father)'. Young children tend to become frightened and confused and very often believe that they are responsible for their parents' break up. It appears that the initial period of divorce and parental separation is profoundly difficult for all children. Even when parents have been caught in severely unhappy marriages, their children usually do not want the divorce to occur and suffer as a result of it. Although it tends to be difficult for all, children of varying ages respond differently.

Younger children tend to worry that their mother will abandon them. They are afraid that they will awaken in the morning and find their mother gone. Acute regression (drinking milk from the bottle, carrying around a security blanket, crying, general fearfulness) are often observed in young children after divorce. Many also become irritable and tearful. One of the most devastating aspects of divorce for children is the sudden removal of a parent – in most cases, the father. They need to be reassured that the departed parent is going to be very much in evidence. This may help in re- establishing their fractured world.

Helping children cope with divorce

- One important factor in helping children cope with divorce is openly communicating with them to express their anger, frustrations, and concerns. Moreover, children need to be adequately prepared for divorce.
- One needs to be honest about explaining the reasons for divorce in a way that is appropriate to the age of the child. You might begin by saying 'may be you have seen that Mama and Papa have not been too happy with each other for some time.' You do not have to elaborate the minute details that the child won't understand.
- It is very important that teachers and parents need to work to keep the children out of the parents' angry battles. Many a times, the discordant scenes that occur before the divorce, continue afterwards. These continual conflicts can be very upsetting to children.
- When one or both parents continue to be distressed, or when the bitter fights continue after the divorce, children find it difficult to deal with the resulting stress and the psychological pain. The child may also be burdened with overwhelming worry about the adult, which soon becomes a chronic part of the child's life.
- Parents should make a special effort to maintain their individual relationships with each child, as this is extremely important to the child's well-being. Generally, it is best to try to maintain a daily routine. A stable routine enables children not to worry about the insecurities of never knowing what each day will bring.
- Try not to criticize or denigrate the other parent in front of the child. Allow the child to grieve for the lost parent. Do not interpret this as loving the lost parent more. It

is just that children miss the parent who is not at home. Allow them to live their pain and work through it as best as they can.

- Parents need not fear openly expressing their emotions. Do not be afraid to cry. Tears are an expression of love. When adults cry in front of children, they are giving their children permission to cry as well. Let children express anger and resentment. This reaction is normal and so they should not be punished for it.

7. Learning From the Growing Child

Am I bringing up my children in the right way? Am I too harsh or too soft with my child? Am I pushing my child too much to excel in his test and examination? Am I shaping the personality of the child in a way that he or she can realize the inherent potential fully? Do I feel stressed dealing with my child? Or am I enjoying nurturing my child?

These are questions that pass through every parent's mind at one time or the other. In fact, this will become more complex if we have a special child or if both parents are working and often feel that they are not spending quality time with their children. Obviously, there is no standard answer that is applicable to all as the context of each home is very different. Yet, it is helpful for every parent and teacher to reflect on such questions. This chapter presents some reflection on helping their parents to observe their child grow and understand them well. The main objective of the chapter is to help parents enjoy listening to their children and participating in the life of their growing child.

1. Are You a Nurturing Father?
2. Are We Consistent with Our Children?
3. What Happens to the Super Kid Syndrome Children?
4. Dos and Don'ts that Shape the Personality of Your Child
5. Dealing with the Dilemma of a Working Mother
6. Accepting and Loving Your Special Child
7. Enjoy Listening to Your Children and Learning about Them

Are You a Nurturing Father?

Recall your interactions with your child during the past one week. How often did you sit with your child to play, to tell stories, or listen to her/him? How many times did you help your child get ready for school or appreciate the effort she/he made to get ready independently? These gestures, although they seem trivial, would help you to be a nurturing parent.

Let us try and imagine three different scenarios that are common in our homes in the evening and through them understand the role of the father in a child's life.

Scene 1:

The father returns home in the evening. No child is to be found around or making a noise. Probably, children in this home are afraid as they may get a shouting if the father's mood is not alright. They have been instructed not to disturb him as he is tired and needs rest.

Scene 2:

The father and the child begin playing with building blocks. The father is instructing the child how to make a building, bridge, tower and many such things. The child wants to use the wooden blocks to play a cooking game, instead, using the blocks as utensils, stove and so on. The father gets upset and tells the child 'You cannot play cooking games with blocks.'

Scene 3:

The child is sitting in the father's lap and is engrossed listening to a story. The child gets off the lap and now both of them are pretending to be animals and are enjoying the sounds and actions of different animals. Simultaneously, the father listens to the child's questions and answers them patiently.

If we try to analyze the first situation, the role of the father in the family is seen as being aloof and distant from the child. It illustrates the traditional image of the father as the bread winner and as the head of the family. His role is to look after the family and the mother's role is to take care of the children and the household work.

In the second situation, there is a change in the role of the father. He is more participatory than the traditional one. In this perspective, the father is perceived to be contributing significantly to the child's development, though on his own terms.

The third situation shows the emergent perspective on fathering, wherein the father takes an active role in his child's rearing. It emphasizes the special role that fathers could play as effective nurturers of their children.

These cases bring forth several questions as the image of the father changes from the traditional image of a breadwinner alone to an emergent role of a nurturing father who participates actively in child rearing. How critical is a father's attitude towards parenting in impacting the psychological adjustment of his children? How does the father influence the role perception and behaviour of the child with respect to the other individuals at home and in later life?

Over the last few decades, there is an increased recognition in society that fathers should participate more in home-making and take an equal share in the parenting role. Fathers are realizing the important contribution they could make to their children's development through the quality of their relationship with the young child, not only as rational and intellectual guides but equally as playmates. It is found that fathers who direct their children's activities in a rational, issue-oriented way and do not arbitrarily impose their will upon children, tend to promote competence as well as self-confidence in their children. Such fathers would also have a great deal of influence on children's psychological well-being. Studies show that authoritarian fathers tend to produce dependent, withdrawn, anxious and dejected children.

The quality of father-child relationships also affects the emotional development and mental health of the child. It will be more effective if fathers develop warm, loving, caring relationships with their children from an early age. Participating in family activities when children are young lays a firm basis for the adolescent years when children seek greater independence. A firm basis between father and child has already been laid. Later, both the father and the growing youth can face the challenges of a changing society without threat or loss of respect of the father by his children. Several studies reveal that warm and accepting fathers tend to have children with high self-esteem while rejecting and neglecting fathers seemed to foster low self-esteem in their children.

The research on relationship between father's absence and the general level of the child's mental adjustment reveals that the loss of the father for any reason is associated with poor adjustment, such as emotional disturbance. It has also been found that absence because of separation, divorce, etc. may have even more severe effects. Children from divorced families are likely to experience difficulties in sex role identification, show lack of self-control, and exhibit anti-social behaviour. Women from homes in which the father had been absent have been found to have difficulty in establishing satisfactory relations with men.

2

Are We Consistent With Our Children?

Five-year-old Parzan is confused. His mother allows him to watch television when she is busy attending to a guest or doing household work. But, at other times, when Parzan wants to watch certain programmes that he likes, he is not allowed to do so.

Ayesha fails to understand her parents' behaviour. They allow her little sister to wear all kinds of clothes. But for her, they are particular about the way she dresses and the way she speaks and interacts with people. She feels discriminated.

There is often a rift between the parents with regard to handling Akash. They have serious differences in their views on children. The mother seems to be quite strict with Akash but very often he gets his way through his father. He has learnt that he can get away with many things in this manner. His mother thinks that being strict with him will make him grow as a disciplined individual.

The above instances are not unusual. Such events take place in almost every home. We consider them to be normal and natural. But how do children perceive and experience such inconsistent behaviour of adults around them?

In Parzan and Ayesha's cases, when they find their parents' inconsistency, they get confused and angry as to why they are allowed to do things selectively and why double standards are followed among siblings.

In general, children do not appreciate differential treatment given to different children at home because of age or gender differences. 'Oh, he is a boy; it is okay if he does not do any household work.' 'You are older; you have to understand your little sister.'

Children do resist such discrimination. However, Ayesha being in the pre-adolescent stage could understand her parents' behaviour if the right reasons had been given and explained to her. But without proper communication, children get confused and begin resenting such differential choices. For every action of ours as parents, if we can carefully read our children's face, we will find a big 'WHY' written on them. We definitely owe an explanation to them for our choices as much as we expect them to give reasons for their behaviour. Many children behave the same way as Akash did. They take advantage of one of the parents when inconsistency is found at their level. This can become a dangerous habit.

It is extremely important to have one voice among parents. Although it is not essential that parents agree entirely about discipline, it is necessary that they support one another in specific instances, such as giving permission to do something, going for a party, watching a certain television programme and so on. Otherwise, children learn to play one parent against the other and are able to do as they please and develop a habit of getting things done the way it suits them. Also, unless discipline is consistent, children are at a loss to know what to do and whom to obey. Children are confused when they learn that not everyone accepts a single rule. Inconsistency between what parents and teachers tell children to do and what they themselves do adds further confusion to children's ideas about what is right and what is wrong.

How do we address this issue as parents?

- o Children consider adults as role models. They try to pattern their own behaviour on the way elders behave around them. It is crucial that all adults who are dealing with children develop a common understanding in handling them, in terms of the rules and limits to be set for their daily routine. On special occasions, it is best that parents sit with their children and advise the jointly.
- o As children grow older, they become perceptive enough to understand that all adults do not react in the same way to similar situations. Adults vary in many small ways as to how they feel comfortable in dealing with young children.

Many children learn that different rules of behaviour operate in different homes. As long as the individual adults are consistent in their own rules, children learn the fact that people are different.

- o Children need to be explained about appropriate behaviour rather than being simply ordered so that they learn to adjust their behaviour accordingly. Never tell the child: 'You cannot understand; just follow what I am telling you.' They may obey you out of fear but that obedience is short-lived.
- o Children learn to respect teachers and parents if they are subjected to consistent values, attitudes and discipline at home and at school. Extreme differences in behaviour patterns prescribed at home and school can be as damaging as between different adults within the home. The young child looks up to the teacher

at school in almost the same as way as she does with her parents.

Children who have experienced consistency in discipline have a stronger motivation to behave according to socially approved standards than those who have received inconsistent discipline. Of course, they will eventually learn to live in a world of differences. But integrity in their personality depends on consistency in the advice and instructions they receive during their early life and in the immediate surroundings of the school and the home. Inconsistency may produce uncertainty, anxiety, and psychosomatic illnesses. It is, therefore, best if the parents are as consistent as possible in responding to their children and open in their communications with them.

3

What Happens to Super Kid Syndrome Children?

The worried young parent asked, 'The other children in my daughter's class have started to go to all kinds of classes – art, dance, music and gymnastics. What shall I do? It is natural for most parents to want their children to be healthy and growing at a normal rate. Some parents try to push their children to grow a little faster and a bit better than the rest – doing more than they are supposed to be doing for their age. They want them to achieve faster in life and become accomplished at an early age. In a nutshell, they want them to be super children. Some of them, who could not do so in their own life, try to achieve it through their children. Many parents, who do not believe in pushing children, end up doing it, fearing that their children may lag behind the rest.

Whatever may be the motivational force for pushing children towards becoming super kids, experts agree that they lose out on their childhood and get burnt out at an early age. The benefits will be short lived and the price too great. What happens to children whose parents impose too much pressure too soon as compared to less pressured children?

- Children often driven by their parents from an early age may lack self-motivation.
- Children who are taught formal learning may have an initial edge but it is quickly lost as other children begin

to catch up. It may be true that some children who are pushed become highly successful as adults but often at the cost of a normal childhood and social life, and sometimes also at the cost of their own happiness.

- They may be advanced in their learning skills in the short run but they are often behind in reasoning, logic and conceptualizing. With early emphasis on structured learning, the skills of creativity often go un- nurtured.
- When they reach formal learning, they are often less enthusiastic about learning than less pressured children, perhaps because the joy and spontaneity get missed out in their learning. They are habituated to please their parents rather than themselves.
- They may have trouble finding their own identity. Children who are pushed to achieve goals set by their parents are deprived of an opportunity to discover their own talents and interests, and what makes them happy.
- Their self-esteem may suffer when they are pushed to tasks beyond their capacities.
- In some cases, they may miss their care-free childhood and this deprivation may stunt their growth as adults.

It is not easy to recognize the warning signs that children give to parents when they are feeling pushed. Some of the symptoms you may look out for could be problems of sleeping or eating, irritability, frequent crying, lack of enthusiasm, inability to play and relate with others, complaints about headaches or stomachaches. Any of these signs require attention. Parents and teachers should help children to ease out their tensions.

Children want adults to listen to them, answer their umpteen numbers of questions, be childlike and play with them. They may not like to be pushed around. Children grow and develop to be the happiest and healthiest even without being pushed around. The important thing is that they should be loved and appreciated for what they are and be allowed to develop at a rate that is appropriate to them. However, it is essential to provide a stimulating and challenging environment where their curiosity to learn and know things around them is nurtured early in life. Follow what children show and say, what interests them and enjoy and satisfy their thirst for knowledge.

Dos and Don'ts that Shape the Personality of Your Child

Five-year-old Reva invariably forgets to take out the lunch box from her bag after she comes home. Every day, her mother reminds her that she has developed a bad habit. She is of course keen on inculcating good hygiene habit in her daughter. But Reva perceives this differently. She considers the daily reminder as unnecessary nagging.

Madhur's parents find that he has been spending, of late, too much time watching television which is affecting his studies and reducing his outdoor play time. After telling him several times to reduce watching television, they mention that they may cut the cable connection. Madhur feels hurt. He thinks that his parents are unreasonable and threatening to punish him. He argues that he would feel isolated when his friends talk about certain T.V. programmes.

For Nisha, the day starts with instructions from her father to get up early to catch the bus: 'Why don't you get up early and get ready? You are always late for the bus.' Her father wants her to be punctual so that she does not miss the bus. This often turns into bitter argument between Nisha and her father. Nisha feels guilty throughout the day for causing such unpleasantness at home.

These are common stories with most parents. As parents, we all have good intentions. We give instructions to our children on dos and don'ts with a view to shaping the personality. We want our children to form good habits, right values and discipline. But do we realize how they feel about it when we keep giving instructions? Why do our children perceive our well-intentioned instructions as being unreasonable, why do they feel that parents try to encroach on their freedom?

Very often, the perception of children and that of adults differs and that creates the daily dichotomy at home. Children often feel that since they have to listen to constant nagging and reprimanding by adults, why should they bother to behave well? Some children also try to be naughty and irritating to attract the attention of adults. They realize that they are attended to when they throw tantrums. They go to extreme extents to provoke you to get the attention which gives them a sense of achievement.

As adults, let us reflect on how we interact with our children. Find out how many times a day we tell our children 'do this' or 'do not do that'. Probably, the answer we get is too often our conversations end up giving such prescriptions. Do we really over-do our instructions? What happens if we do not say anything to our children for a couple of days? Probably, they would feel that we do not care about them. Nisha would tell her father: 'You do not care if I get up early and catch the bus in time!' Children want you to take care of them. The question, therefore, is not to stop guiding our children but to pause and ask ourselves: Am I over reacting? How do I balance the 'dos and don'ts' part with other kinds of communication with the children?

What can we do as parents?

Of course there is no perfect way of dealing with children and their behaviour. But it is helpful to keep certain points as guideposts while dealing with them. This may help you but there are no readymade solutions.

- Try to place yourself in the shoes of the child. For example, Madhur was facing his own dilemma. As adults we are worried about acceptance of our children by other adults. For children, acceptance by parents is paramount but their own peer group acceptance is equally important. Would it not help if you talk to your child and understand his/her own predicament?
- Never say 'I am doing this only for your good; what do I gain from it?' They do not doubt your intentions at all. They value your words as much as you have their interests in view. But such statements are interpreted by children as unwanted pressure tactics and curtailing of their freedom.
- Examine if your way of communicating your intentions needs be changed. Could 'instructions' be changed to friendly 'advice'? Begin the day with positive strokes. Unpleasant interactions in the morning will linger with you as much as with your child throughout the day.

Finally, remember that the young child lives in today's world. But we are trying to shape their personality for tomorrow's world. Some frictions and tensions are part of this 'growing up' and 'bringing up'. Let us enjoy our life with our children as they grow up with a sense of accommodation and flexibility.

5

Dealing With the Dilemma of a Working Mother

'I can't help feeling guilty – especially when I see other mothers at home.' These are the words of Riya's mother. Of course, this is not the agony of just one mother but of many mothers who work leaving their children at home. Women taking up work outside home and making a career is becoming a common feature of our society. This they do for a variety of reasons ranging from the compulsion of earning a livelihood for the family to creating an opportunity for intellectual stimulation or simply to remain engaged in productive work. A generation ago, mothers were expected to be housewives and taking care of their children at home. But the situation has begun to change significantly. Child rearing in urban families is becoming a participatory activity; it is no more confined only to the mother. But there is still a long way to go. Working mothers continue to bear the dual duty of primary care giver to the child and also work outside like any other professional. Should she really feel guilty for this?

In this context, the mother is compelled to make critical choices. It is difficult to judge what is right or wrong – staying at home or working outside. Probably, the important issue is 'how to balance work and home'. One need not always feel that decision to work will compromise the child's future.

Studies show that children whose mothers work do not necessarily suffer emotional scars or tend to be any less adjusted than children of mothers who stay at home. They perform on par both socially and academically. One should feel fortunate to be the part of a generation of women who have more than one option open and be able to select that which makes them happy. In the same way, a woman who wants to stay home with her child should not be forced into employment out of home. Anyone choosing to stay at home need not feel less of a person but feel fortunate to have the luxury of affording that choice. If staying home with your child feels like the right choice for you, enjoy doing it.

Whether a parent chooses to stay home or go out to work, a certain amount of doubt is normal. No one, man or woman, need be embarrassed about being a full time parent. Full time parenting demands as much dedication and hard work as any other occupation. The problem is with the society that is yet to acknowledge this reality.

As mentioned earlier, many working parents feel guilty about not attending to their children adequately. But this is relative to your own expectation. It is important to understand that simply spending most of your time with children does not ensure a good parent-child relationship. In fact, the relationship may get affected by too much nagging or doting on them.

Therefore, instead of worrying on who spends more time, it is important to reflect on how you spend that time with your child – talking, listening, and playing. The focus should be on ensuring that the child feels secure and well attended. For this, you have to ensure that the time you spend with the child enhances the emotional bonding. You don't have to be alone in this; both father and mother have to complement each other in bringing up the child.

There are creative ways to keep in touch with your children when you are away at work –

- o A routine is comforting to both children and parents. Do certain chores together as a part of the routine. For example, snuggling together in the bed with your child before getting up from the bed in the morning, breakfast together, a lunchtime phone call, playing or walking.
- o Leave a note for your child. Avoid saying 'I miss you'. This may upset the child. The note can be in the form of a picture, drawing or something that the person who looks after child can read out to the child.
- o Stay in touch when the child comes home from the school. A brief chat could help the child to feel secure. Talk about what you have been doing and ask about how the day was?
- o Occasionally, you can take your child to your work place so that the child can get familiar with your work and your colleagues too. Explain to your child what you do and how you do your work. Make it clear that being out of sight does not put him/her out of your mind. Make sure to point out the drawings or photographs that you carry with you or you have displayed in your work area.
- o If your work place is nearby, try having lunch together sometimes. Discontinue it if it creates a problem getting back to your work.

- A generation ago, fathers were expected to be the sole breadwinners. But today in a growing number of families, the father stays at home and parents the child by choice. If the nature of your work permits, you can work from home, if you are keen not to be physically separated from your child, there are many possibilities one can think of.

6

Accepting and Loving Your Special Child

Each child is unique. Children, who have been brought up in the same environment, sharing the same physical and emotional challenges, are never exactly alike. Thus, no two children are same and neither are their needs. It is just that some children have more special needs and challenges than others. Yet children of same age, in their early years, would have so many things in common that we tend to overlook this basic truth of differences in needs and challenges. Consequently, we as parents fail to notice if something is unusual about our children. In case of children with special needs, early recognition of their special conditions and speedy intervention are extremely important. It is not just observing their special condition but also learning the cause of the condition that is equally important. This would help us understand and accept the child without any feeling of guilt. It is important to know whether the special needs are a result of environmental factors such as a simple allergy, a minor birth defect, or a condition that severely impairs normal functioning. The well-being of children with special needs depends, of course, on the kind of professional help they get. At the same time, parents' participation and that extra attention they get could make a world of difference to the quality of their lives.

What can parents do?

- It is natural for parents to begin thinking that they are responsible for their child's condition. It is also natural that we do not easily accept the reality that our child has special needs. It is important to accept the condition for your own sake and for the sake of your child and your family.

- It is desirable that both parents get involved in the medical consultations so that they get firsthand information, which will help in dealing with day to day issues. It also helps in reducing the burden of one of the parents and making the whole experience of coming to terms with the reality less stressful. If you are a single parent, try to get a friend or grandparents to be with you in this.
- It is important to know and update yourself about the child's condition and the latest developments in medical technology. This may include everything from surgery to new types of support equipment, from correcting squint in the eye or impaired hearing to a computer that can help physically challenged children play games, do homework, or write to express what you speak.
- Show your love unconditionally with patience and understanding as you do with any other children – like hugging, offering a helping hand or sharing moments of pleasure and pain. Seek professional help if you feel frustrated and find it difficult to be normal. This is critical as sometimes your frustration may unconsciously lead to verbal or physical abuse.
- Try to lead a normal family life. There is a possibility of either neglecting normal children at home or not attending to the needs of the special child, and striking a balance is not an easy job.
- Set limits for discipline according to the child's development. Being over permissive or over indulgent

towards a special child won't help. It may further affect his/her development.

- Every child needs appreciation, so do children with special needs. Look beyond the condition for qualities or traits that make your child special – a beautiful smile, a kind heart, a loving and affectionate nature, and so on. This will help in developing a positive outlook for both you and your child.
- We often deprive ourselves of simple pleasures of life. We feel guilty at even the thought of having fun. This is not warranted. Taking a lighter approach to life can help you and your child deal with the condition and help you think positively.
- Take help from family members, professionals and other support groups who have the experience of dealing with special children. This will help in coping with the needs of your child and of the other family members, and in organizing your time without feeling guilty.

For majority of the children with special needs, love, support and appropriate therapy can improve the prognosis dramatically. For this, you have to accept the realities of the child's limitations and recognize what she will or will not be able to do. The more accepting you are of your child, the more self-accepting she/he will grow up to be. Accepting your child's condition does not mean that you should not make every effort to help your child reach his/her maximum potential. Rather, such acceptance has to be accompanied by a positive outlook for the future and constant efforts to improve the physical and emotional comfort levels of your child.

Enjoy Listening to Your Children and Learning about Them

Young children keep talking or drawing. Sometimes this is in response to an external stimulation and sometimes they even indulge in self-talk or random doodling. But do we listen to them? Do we look at what they draw? Most often these appear trivial and insignificant; at best we treat them as funny and amusing. Is child talk only worth that much? Perhaps, we are grossly undervaluing our children. Every time they talk, they are communicating very significant messages about themselves and their surroundings. Their words invariably hold a mirror to their evolving personality. What is needed is patience and curiosity on our part. They express with a different logic; a logic which is different from the one that an adult uses to communicate. In fact, they could contain very profound value statements on life, their likes and dislikes, and their view of the world as they see. Further, it unravels the story of their intellectual and emotional development, the way they think, and understand the world around them, their sensitivity and relationships with things in the environment, and the way they perceive people around them. It is really fascinating listening to them if we have the patience to understand the idiom in which they are trying to communicate to us.

Let us look at the following three real life incidents recorded and illustrated by teachers. These are exactly what the children spoke in response to specific events and what the teachers recorded faithfully as the latter found meaning in their words. Young children with their curious and inquisitive mind have many questions and interesting solutions too!

1

Most people donate their eyes at the time they die.

Then how will they be able to see in heaven?

2

Why didn't you come to school yesterday?

I had fever 200°

You cannot have a temperature of 200°

One hand 100 + other hand 100 = 200?

3

The first incident is about a child who wondered at what would happen to those who donate their eyes! How would they see in heaven! For the child who can only fathom concrete objects, life in heaven is as concrete as on earth.

The second illustrative incident is about a child who said he had got a fever of 200°! What logic! It is so interesting to understand the way children think. For a while, the teacher did not understand what the child was trying to tell in response to her question on how high was the fever. The child explained: 'My mother checked in each arm and said in each case it was 100°. Together does it not become 200°?' This may appear strange to an adult. But for the child, treating the two measurements as two different events and adding them therefore seemed more logical. This reflects the typical thinking style of a child of concrete operational stage. At this stage, children's abilities are limited to manipulating, playing, and exploring with concrete objects and materials. Parents and teachers have to have patience in dealing with the child's own logic and should not treat the answer as illogical and wrong.

The third illustrative incident should be an eye opener for the adult world on values. Very early in life, we introduce our children to the world of competition. What does the child have to say? The child was participating in a running race and got the third position. The teacher observed that the child had slowed down while running and asked why she did not run fast. The child's reply stunned the teacher, 'But my friends would have lagged behind. I was waiting for them.' What an idea on friendship, cooperation and competition! Only children can think differently.

Listening to how children describe their own drawings could also reflect their imageries and the way they relate with other objects and individuals in their real life. Look at the drawings of children on 'Myself and My Family'.

The self portrait of the child clearly shows how the child perceives herself. Further, the details in the drawing reflect the ability of the child to capture the ideas graphically. Observe the placement of family members in the drawing on 'My Family'. It possibly indicates the child's location of different people at home in her own personal space. Do we ever think that the child also conceives of a personal space as we adults do? Children construct their knowledge through these means and methods which are natural choices of communicating by and with others. The message is very simple and straightforward. Let us enjoy listening

to and observing our children as they speak and express themselves through other means. They not only tell us about themselves but they can also be communicating profound messages on their view of life and its surroundings. They can hold a mirror to their own growing and developing personality.

VIII. The Child and the School

Very often, parents feel that getting children into the school early will help them learn more and faster. But before we get children into school, it is important to assess if they are ready to go to school and benefit from the organized activities in the school. Parents also need to ask themselves whether they are ready to be away from their child for several hours every day. It is important that parents prepare themselves emotionally to send their children to school and also prepare their children for the new kind of life they have to spend. Further, it is also important for parents to understand the relationship between school and home and the child and school environment. This chapter discusses how this understanding is critical for everyone so that the pressure of schooling does not damage the rhythm of development of the child, which may in turn lead to behavioural disorders. In their enthusiasm to get their children ahead of others in school, parents may fail to notice the aberrations in their children's behaviour. It is indeed important that early school experiences provide a sense of security and self-esteem to the child. The chapter discusses how parental understanding is central for ensuring a secure learning environment for the child.

1. Your Child Goes to School: Are You Ready?
2. Danger of Pushing Children in Early Years of Schooling
3. Working With Children at Home
4. Is My Child Developing Alright?

Your Child Goes to School: Are You Ready?

It is a common sight to find some children crying and clinging to their parents for a couple of days after joining the school. You will also find children like Janu telling other children who are crying on their first day of schooling. 'Do not cry, your mother will come to pick you up.'

What can parents do to make this transition of the child's life at home to school smooth and pleasant, free from anxiety and distress? How do we prepare our children for entry into school? Here are some suggestions. All parents have their own childhood memories, both pleasant and unpleasant, about school. A child's entry into a school brings out the feelings they had when they started school themselves, particularly, feelings associated with unpleasant experiences, which have left an emotional scar. Therefore, in remembering their own school experiences parents may have apprehensions about their child's new experience. Let us be careful that we do not influence the child's behaviour by projecting our own childhood experiences.

By the time the first child begins school, most parents have been away from the educational system for a number of years. It will be helpful for parents to re-acquaint themselves with the educational system and the arrangements for schooling before the child enters the school.

Very often we find that the anxiety associated with a child's entry to school is not just his/hers alone. Parents, especially mothers, may experience some anxiety of their own over their child's separation. Mothers need to separate their anxiety from that of the child's. The young child is very perceptive to parents' anxiety and gets influenced by it.

- Treat the first day of going to school in a normal fashion as part of daily life without much high drama and special celebration. Talk about the school the child is going to go, teachers, and play and other interesting activities as an extension of the experiences and activities at home.
- Do answer questions children ask about the school and tell them what to expect there. They may like to know how long they will be in the school and who will come to pick them up. Working parents need to explain the arrangement made for the child to go to school and return home.
- Life in a new place is likely to create stress and anxiety in some children. This is not unusual. Talking to them will help reduce their anxiety. Encourage them to express their feelings about the school freely.
- Some children might have already attended the play school. For them, going to school may not be a problem. But some of them may still have some problem of adjustment to the new setting. In such situations, parents should talk to them about the difference in the environment.
- Children who are secure feel less anxious about the new situation. Parents need to reassure the child. This

will help them to adjust faster. Gradually, children feel comfortable away from home. They learn to trust their teacher and make friends with others. They realize that interesting and exciting things happen in the school. They will soon begin to enjoy coming to school.

You will also relax and enjoy observing the growth and development of your child under the emerging partnership between school and home.

Danger of Pushing Children in Early Years of Schooling

It is natural for us as parents to want our children to grow and develop well. For instance, every parent is eager to see her child stand up and walk. But we also know that we have to wait for that to happen. You cannot make a six-month-old child to walk. You cannot expect a one-year-old child run fast. We need to tell ourselves: 'There is a time for everything; we have to be patient and follow nature's pace and pattern of growth and development.' What applies to physical development is equally relevant to intellectual activities. There is mounting evidence from scientific studies that children should not be pushed to writing and arithmetic when they come to pre-school classes. You have to wait till they come to primary school years just as you wait for a child to walk on her own.

Apart from research studies, field realities also indicate psychological damage to children if they are pushed to perform when they are not physically and mentally ready to do various activities. Early head start in giving education does not mean downward extension of primary school chores. There is a misconception that if reading and writing skills are given earlier, children will gain an advantage in their later learning. This is as wrong an assumption as believing that a child who is helped to walk a month earlier than normal would be a better walker or runner than other children who acquire this in their normal course of growth and development.

Rather, the child helped prematurely to walk may inadvertently develop deformities of gait and posture in coping with the pressure. Similarly, if children are pushed too early to reading, writing and arithmetic, they lose their curiosity to explore the world around them, stop being naturally creative, and may become anxious and fearful.

All children pass through similar patterns of growth and development. The rate of development may vary but not the steps and processes. What happens to children if we interfere in their natural process of intellectual development and learning? For instance, can we teach mathematical operations like 'What does 1 and 2 make?' to a four or five-year-old child? While this may appear very elementary to the adult, it involves establishing formal and abstract linkages which are totally unfamiliar to preschool children.

They live in a world of concrete objects and operations but the above problem uses formal language of arithmetic and does not refer to particular objects or entities. It is not that a preschool child does not have any knowledge of numbers. But in this apparently simple problem they are encountering a novel code, and are required to find a link between the formal language of arithmetic and their existing number knowledge. Preschool children cannot create these links for themselves. Forcing them to acquire these would make them lose interest and confidence in using their own number knowledge capabilities, which are rooted in concrete objects.

These concepts remain non-comprehended by children – a mental burden. If such experiences are repeated over a period, children begin to suffer from what is known as the load of non-comprehension. Eventually, children begin to show signs of disinterest in school learning altogether and often get branded as dull and slow learners.

Preschool education is essentially a programme of school readiness. Most learning in early years takes place through play and through a variety of experiences like storytelling, role play, music and movement, and free exploration. Parents who push children to formal learning through memorization of alphabets and multiplication tables leave them with a perpetual feeling of inadequacy and take away the opportunity to develop the right perception of self-concept.

Many children under pressure develop habit disorders like nail biting, bed wetting and thumb sucking. In extreme cases, children undergoing academic stress may suffer from chronic muscular pains, diarrhoea, headaches and stomach aches. Such children face the prospect of 'burn-out' by the time they reach primary classes. Even children, who succeed well in their studies, may continue to carry mental stresses and strains throughout their life.

What should we do as parents and teachers?

- o Try to fit into children's world and not fit them into the adult's world. Think and look at the world from their perspective. That way, we will be able to enjoy their childhood.
- o Provide them opportunities to explore and experiment with things around them and help them discover the world. This gives them a sense of achievement and happiness.
- o Provide them a sense of belongingness and security so that they become confident individuals. Early school experiences should reinforce this feeling in children.
- o Accept their way of thinking and give them conceptual freedom to think differently so that they become creative persons.

3

Working with Children at Home

From the early years, children need opportunities to play creatively and engage in work experiences. They learn to share, to take turns, and to take care of things. They gain experiences which teach them self-reliance, independence and co-operation. They need experiences to explore, experiment, and to exercise their imagination. Parents can help their children to develop such behaviour pattern in a natural fashion. For this, they have to demonstrate this and work with their children.

Working together around the house encourages the feeling of family unity and oneness. There are many household jobs that can be shared by everyone. Dusting, cleaning, putting things away, shopping, cooking, gardening are some of the possibilities. Children should have the choice and be allowed to do some of the things they enjoy doing. Disagreeable jobs should be shared by everyone including the grown-ups. It is more fun when parents and children do things together and laugh and joke while doing them. This kind of working together helps children grow healthy both physically and emotionally.

Reading together, talking together, watching a television programme with an educational value, and perhaps, following it with a discussion are examples of activities that promote togetherness. Other examples include trips to the museum, the art gallery, the zoo, the airport, the post office, watching a house being built, and going for a nature walk.

Talking and listening

Talk about the book you are reading or the work you are doing. Ask questions, encourage your child to talk and listen attentively to what he or she is saying. Talking and listening to each other is at the heart of language development. The grasp of language is the high road to learning to think. Thinking, talking, and close, friendly relationships go a long way in a child's development. Your conversation with your child is as important as the actual work you do together.

How do we work together at home?

Enjoyment and relaxation

Try to see that your child feels relaxed and free from pressure. It is only at home that children can be given opportunities to learn at their own speed. This sense of relaxation you will want to feel too when you are bothered by your work or preoccupied.

Interest and purpose

Your attitudes are the ones your children are most likely to adopt. You are providing a model for your child as far as learning is concerned. If it is fun and interesting for you then it is for your child as well. Purpose is closely linked with interest. Children want and need to master things around them, and this gives them a powerful motivation to learn what that world is about.

Praise

Praise your child often – for anything that is worthy of praise. All children need encouragement to boost their confidence and help them to take the next step forward.

Never too long at a time

When you sit down for a learning session with your child, work only for short periods at a time. You will find that ten to twenty minutes may be needed for reading activities but five might be enough for learning spellings or doing an arithmetic problem – especially for young children. A few minutes of learning experience is worth hours of boring struggle, which only puts children off learning.

Learning by doing

Whatever you are trying to teach your child, ensure there is some activity that would help to make the information real. Instead of just talking about metric measurements, measure the furniture or if you find a good story, act it out together, helping the child to make a model that demonstrates the principle of lever.

Parents need to know more than the general pattern of children's growth and the kinds of behaviour to expect at various ages. If they are to understand their own child they must know and believe that each child is different from every other child. Each child needs the feeling that he is well accepted and is part of the family. He needs to feel that his ideas, hopes and problems are important.

Is My Child Developing Alright?

'Is my child doing what he or she is supposed to at this age?' – is a question that is often asked by the parents. The answer to this is to observe the child's developmental indicators. These indicators help adults to get a clearer perspective on the child's development. It is very important to look closely at their progress from time to time, to check that their abilities are growing; their mastery of skills are normal according to their age and stage of development; and to note if there is little or lower than expected change in any aspect of development.

If a child is progressing normally, then a check of her abilities will indicate her progress in different areas of development. If a child is not progressing well this regular check can be the basis for planning some special time with the child to help in achieving the mastery of skills and competencies. Observations of most children are likely to show that their development is progressing well, with no problems. In this situation, adults should make sure that appropriate play activities are available that encourage her to extend her abilities further and offer a feeling of challenge.

The basic developmental indicators are:

Satisfaction of basic needs – sleep, rest and food

- o Does your child sleep well?
- o If she takes proper rest, she is fresh to get on with life and remain cheerful.

- Does your child eat properly? Does she eat with appetite? Occasional skipping of meals or refusal of food is normal.

Toilet training

- Does she have bowel/bladder control? Occasional 'accidents' are alright, particularly under special circumstances such as excessive intake of liquids or intestinal upset.

Expression of emotions

- Does she express a range of emotions as joy, anger, sorrow, grief, enthusiasm, excitement, frustration, love, and affection? A child whose emotions don't vary – who is always angry or sour or enthusiastic – may be in trouble.

Relating to others – adults and children

- Does your child relate to her peer group? Make friends? Play with friends? Does she find difficulty in making friends? Children who do not mix with others or are fearful of their peers may require attention.

Curiosity to know the world around

- Is she curious to know about the things around her? You must have observed children asking questions about everything they see. They always have questions of what, how and why. This is an indication of their ability to observe, explore and make sense about what they see and experience. They are interested in everything around them.

Attention span

- o Does she concentrate on any given activity for a duration of ten minutes to start with? Is she distracted and not able to concentrate at all? You must have observed some children playing for a long period of time. They enjoy what they are doing while others keep getting distracted and flipping from one thing to the other.

You do not have to seek a special time or method to observe your child on these behaviour patterns. Keep an eye on these aspects as you interact with and observe your child in the normal course of the day. It is most unlikely that you will fail to notice unusualness in the rhythm of behaviour, if any. Definitely, you do not have to make any written observations to identify if your child is growing normally. But you need to be alert. Some children may even orally express their predicaments to an adult close to them. When and how may vary. For instance, almost all young children respond well to spending time with an adult who is important to them. The important adult may be a parent, relative, caregiver, or anyone else with whom the child has a significant relationship.

Epilogue

Parenthood is a unique gift of nature to all of us. The birth of a child is celebrated in every family. Observing a child growing from infancy to a mature young person is a very special experience. The day our little child began speaking simple words, began crawling and sitting up, could stand up and walk with support – each of these milestones in the life of our child gets etched in our memory as joyous moments. As the child grows, the demands of the child vary as much as the expectations of the parents. The home environment does not remain the same as the toddler becomes a grown up boy or girl and then acquires an increasingly independent voice as an adolescent and a young adult.

In fact, life does not remain static around the child. We, the parents and other adults around the child, also evolve with the child, in our personal relationships as well as our work lives. It is indeed a unique life space that gets created around us and the growing child. Who would not like to enjoy the experience of parenting? But it is worth reflecting on 'How much do we all enjoy parenting our children?' Not every one of us would have the same answer to this. The real question before us is 'How do we ensure that parenting becomes joyous and satisfying?' There is no standard answer. One simple principle seems to be that we can enjoy our parenthood only when our child enjoys childhood. We have to ask ourselves 'Is my child happy with the way I am bringing her up?' Difficult to answer! After all, a small child will not speak or tell you these things. But parents do make out if the child is enjoying the experience of growing up or not. This ability to make out if the child is happy with oneself and the surroundings is the crux of sensitive parenting.

Is parenting solely a relationship between a parent and a child or a mother and a child? Sensitive parenting has to encompass the whole environment in which the child is evolving, in particular, the immediate life space surrounding the child. This includes parents, siblings and other adults at home including the physical environment. Creating such a comfort zone around a growing child in a sensitive manner requires peace and harmony at home.

As the child grows up, the world around expands. New and significant actors enter the child's life. This includes an expanding peer group – boys and girls, often influencing the child's thinking and behaviour. A whole new world gets added as the child steps into the school – a new set of friends and adults (teachers). With this, arise new expectations. Adjusting to the new environment of the school and negotiating the world of new people and new set of activities is a gradual process. Handholding by parents with full understanding of the changing expectations arising from the new relationships and activities is critical for the healthy development of the child. Yet, for the child, the home continues to be a special place and the child expects parents to continue occupying a significant place in this expanding world.

How and how much do we succeed in harmonising the world at home and the expanding world outside will determine how joyful childhood will be for the child and parenting for us. Outside influences, in particular, the peer group, may bring unexpected demands, some of which we may disapprove of. Yet, these are only passing phases. In the long run, it is not material comfort alone that will make a child enjoy childhood. Rather, it is the feeling of security arising out of sensitive, understanding and trustful parenting that will make a child feel happy growing up.